EVERYDAY ANSWERS

EVERYDAY ANSWERS

TRUE STORIES ABOUT GOD'S PRESENCE IN OUR LIVES

JAY A. PARRY

DESERET
BOOK
SALT LAKE CITY, UTAH

Also in this series:

Everyday Miracles: True Stories about God's Hand in Our Lives

Everyday Heroes: True Stories of Ordinary People Who Made a Difference

Visit us at deseretbook.com

Library of Congress Cataloging-in-Publication Data

Everyday answers : true stories about God's presence in our lives / [compiled by] Jay A. Parry.

p. cm.

Includes bibliographical references and indexes.

ISBN 1-57008-982-5 (pbk.)

1. Christian life—Mormon authors. 2. Miracles. I. Parry, Jay A. II. Title.

BX8656.E94 2003

248.4'893—dc21 2003010614

Printed in the United States of America 72076-7096

Publishers Printing, Salt Lake City, UT

10 9 8 7 6 5 4 3 2 1

CONTENTS

INTRODUCTION

Few invitations are repeated so often in the scriptures as the invitation to pray. "Ask, and it shall be given you," the Lord said (Matthew 7:7). "Whatsoever ye shall ask the Father in my name, which is right, believing that ye shall receive, behold it shall be given unto you" (3 Nephi 18:20; for other such promises see, for example, Matthew 21:22; Luke 11:9; 1 Nephi 15:11; Enos 1:15; Mosiah 4:21; 3 Nephi 14:7; 27:29; Moroni 7:26; D&C 4:7; 42:3; 88:63).

We read in the scriptures and have seen in our lives the many marvelous ways in which this promise is fulfilled. The sick have been healed and the dead raised, financial disasters have been averted, marriages have been saved, wayward children have been reached and retrieved, hearts have been changed, critical guidance has been given about marriage choices and careers. When we need the Lord in big things, when we seek him in humility and "with real intent" (Moroni 10:4), he is ready to answer us.

But so is he ready to help us with little things. He gives help with difficulties in relationships, peace and comfort in the face of adversity, help with overcoming even small problems of worthiness or obedience, answers to many questions about many things, help in finding lost keys or a misplaced legal document, help with ideas to help us better conquer our everyday problems.

Amulek counseled us to be prayerful about every aspect of our lives—not just the big things but the "everyday" things as well. "Cry unto [God] for mercy; for he is mighty to save," he said. "Yea, humble yourselves, and continue in prayer unto him.

"Cry unto him when ye are in your fields, yea, over all your flocks.

"Cry unto him in your houses, yea, over all your household, both morning, mid-day, and evening.

"Yea, cry unto him against the power of your enemies.

"Yea, cry unto him against the devil, who is an enemy to all righteousness.

"Cry unto him over the crops of your fields, that ye may prosper in them.

"Cry over the flocks of your fields, that they may increase.

"But this is not all; ye must pour out your souls in your closets, and your secret places, and in your wilderness.

"Yea, and when you do not cry unto the Lord, let your hearts be full, drawn out in prayer unto him continually for your welfare, and also for the welfare of those who are around you" (Alma 34:18–27).

In private counsel to his son Helaman, Alma emphasized the same principles, underscoring that we should seek the Lord's guidance and help in all aspects of our lives, large and small: "Cry unto God for all thy support; yea, let all thy doings be unto the Lord, and whithersoever thou goest let it be in the Lord; yea, let all thy thoughts be directed unto the Lord; yea, let the affections of thy heart be placed upon the Lord forever.

"Counsel with the Lord in all thy doings, and he will direct thee for good; yea, when thou liest down at night lie down unto the Lord, that he may watch over you in your sleep; and when thou risest in the morning let thy heart be full of thanks unto God; and if ye do these things, ye shall be lifted up at the last day" (Alma 37:36–37).

This counsel was repeated in our time by President Gordon B. Hinckley, when he said in general conference:

"I offer a plea that each of us will seek to live closer to the Lord and to commune with Him more frequently and with increased faith.

"Fathers and mothers, pray over your children. Pray that they may be shielded from the evils of the world. Pray that they may grow in faith and knowledge. Pray that they may be directed toward lives that will be profitable and good. Husbands, pray for your wives. Express unto the Lord your gratitude for them and plead with Him in their behalf. Wives, pray for your husbands. Many of them walk a very difficult road with countless problems and great perplexities. Plead with the Almighty that they may be guided, blessed, protected, inspired in their righteous endeavors.

"Pray for peace in the earth, that the Almighty who governs the universe will stretch forth His hand and let His Spirit brood upon the people, that the nations may not rage one against another. Pray for the weather. We have floods in one area and drought in another. I am satisfied that if enough prayers ascend to heaven for moisture upon the land, the Lord will answer those prayers for the sake of the righteous. . . .

"Pray for wisdom and understanding as you walk the difficult paths of your lives. If you are determined to do foolish and imprudent things, I think the Lord will not prevent you. But if you seek His wisdom and follow the counsel of the impressions that come to you, I am confident that you will be blessed.

"Let us be a prayerful people" ("Benediction," *Ensign*, May 2003, 99–100).

Of course, not all prayers are answered in the way we would hope. Sometimes keys remain lost; sometimes wayward children remain lost—not because the Lord and earthly loved ones don't reach out, but because of their own expression of agency. Sometimes financial problems don't end in a miracle but in bankruptcy, and that to worthy people. Sometimes we plead for guidance and the Lord answers, "You may choose." Always he blesses us in his wisdom, and always he sends his love to all who will receive it.

This book collects many true stories of answers to prayers. For the most part, these are stories of help the Lord gives to those who seek him in everyday matters. The great matters of life and death, both temporally and spiritually, are not the subject of this book; instead, we have gathered many sweet and powerful accounts of everyday Saints who have sought the Lord and received his assistance in the many challenges they face in their day-to-day lives. A few of these stories do involve major miracles, but in each instance they are presented with the smaller blessings the Lord is pleased to give us as we seek him.

Some of the names of those who have written stories have been changed to protect their anonymity. Some names and other details within some of the stories have been changed for the same purpose. Otherwise, all aspects of these stories are true, testimonies of the love and power of our God, who ever desires to lift and help and bless his children.

I would like to thank those who have assisted in helping this book become a reality. I am grateful for those who helped in different stages of the creation process, including Dee Ann Barrowes, Norma Barrowes, Tandea Ford, Latrisha Gordon, Annaka Palacios, and Vicki Parry. I thank the excellent professionals at Deseret Book for their role in making this a published book—Cory Maxwell, Jana Erickson, Jack M. Lyon, Janna DeVore, Tom Hewitson, Kent Minson, Doreen McKnight, and Christine Neilson. And I thank those many faithful Saints who wrote their experiences with a desire to share with others the goodness of God in their lives.

The effectual fervent prayer of a righteous man availeth much.

JAMES 5:16

"WHAT ARE YOU DOING IN CAIRO?"

JACK R. CHRISTIANSON

In 1983 my wife and I traveled to Israel, Italy, and Egypt with a study group. When we arrived in Cairo, it was just after midnight. We were all tired, and the heat, even at that early hour, was intense. After finding our luggage and going through customs, we looked for the buses that would transport us to our hotel—a simple task in America, but not in Egypt. We were surrounded by crowds of people. Even though it was early, hundreds stood outside the airport waiting to see, barter, and associate with Americans. I had never seen anything like it. Ropes were placed on each side of the walkway to control the crowds, but it didn't work. No one could see where to go. Finally our group leader picked my wife and me and another couple to be the bus search party. We were assigned to take our shopping-cart-type luggage carriers and make our way through the throng of people. Once we found the buses, we were to get into a position where everyone else could see us, and then the rest of the group would gather at that spot.

The other couple led the way. Melanie and I followed them

with our cart, almost fighting our way through the crowd. Even the sounds were annoying. People were saying short phrases in English, probably with little knowledge of the meaning. They grabbed at our clothes and tried to get us to trade everything we had, from pens to tennis shoes, for small "Egyptian artifacts."

It took us a few minutes, but we finally made it past the sea of people to the parking lot. We found the buses and were greeted by a resident member of the Church. I then found a cement guardrail pole, two or three feet high. I climbed up on top so I would be visible to the rest of the group. My wife held my ankles so I would not slip off. When I located our group I began to wave my arms so they could see me. I'm sure I looked like a large, awkward bird trying to fly.

While balancing on top of the post, waving my arms, I heard an American calling my name. It was difficult at first to discern it above the noise of the buses and the crowds, but I was certain someone was calling me. I looked around for the source and saw two young men running toward me through the parking lot. They were carrying suitcases in each hand. I didn't recognize either one of them, but they definitely knew me, and one of them continued to call my name.

I jumped from the post and then helped my partner up. He began to wave his arms as I had, and I walked toward the two young men.

"Are you Jack Christianson?" one of them asked.

"Yes," I replied. "Who are you?"

"You were one of my dad's missionaries in the Arizona Holbrook Mission, years ago."

"Ron Felt?" I questioned.

"Yes. You remember me?"

"Of course I do. What are you doing in Cairo at 2:00 in the morning?"

Tears came to both their eyes. Ron briefly explained that he and his friend had left their young wives at home and come to Egypt to study at the University of Cairo International School of Business. But there had been a mix-up, and no one was at the air terminal to meet them. They had no way of getting to the city, no place to sleep, no way to communicate with anyone to explain their situation. They were scared, to say the least. They had been there about eight hours, doing everything they could to solve their problem. Nothing worked. They had begun to worry about being caught helplessly in Egypt. They worried that they'd be unable to accomplish their goal. They even got to the point of wondering if they'd ever get home.

They had finally decided to go outside of the terminal and find a place to kneel down and pray. They said they had found a quiet place, knelt down, and explained their situation to the Lord. They pleaded for help. In this case, the heavens were opened. They didn't simply hear a voice. They didn't see a vision. They simply got up, walked around the corner of the terminal, and saw an American standing on a guardrail post, waving his arms. Ron had said, "I think that's one of my dad's missionaries." It was.

I introduced the young men to the resident member of the Church. He took them to his home for a couple of days, helped them get a place to live, and helped settle the problem with the university.

The heavens were penetrated, and two humble elders kneeling on the pavement outside an airport terminal communed with Deity. Was it coincidence that I, the only member of our group who had served in the Arizona Holbrook Mission, was chosen to find the buses? I don't think so. I believe these young men were worthy to penetrate the heavens and that they were willing and able to try. The Lord knew it too, and arranged for me to participate in a simple, but profound, experience.

The power to draw upon the heavens is real. Sometimes the Lord answers very directly, sometimes indirectly. But I do know he answers.

Christianson, *What's So Bad about Being Good?* 103–5.

O Lord, wilt thou grant unto us that we may have success in bringing them again unto thee in Christ. Behold, O Lord, their souls are precious.

ALMA 31:34–35

LOVE THROUGH HIS TOES

MELODIE CHILD

My son was slipping away from me, and I felt helpless. I had done everything I knew how to do, and it wasn't enough. Paul was leaving behind some of the values of the gospel and the blessings he could receive by keeping those values. I knew about the teachings of the prophets and had tried to help and love Paul according to those teachings. And yet he was withdrawing from me and making other choices.

I felt the distance as, one by one, things that had kept us close were let go, things like praying together, going to church together, playing together, eating together. With every withdrawing, I watched and cried inside and, when no one was looking, I cried outside as well.

With despair I pleaded with my Heavenly Father to tell me what to do. I needed divine guidance. I could not stand this alone. I prayed again and again.

Then, one day, I thought I understood an answer, but the

answer seemed ridiculous. Had I understood the Spirit correctly? It seemed to be saying, "Keep cutting his toenails."

"Keep cutting his toenails?" I wondered.

"Yes," came the answer.

Ever since Paul was a little tiny boy I had cut his toenails. This was one thing I still had. He had not rejected this small act. It was the one way I could still touch him, and in those few minutes every week or two I could pour love through my hands into my son through his toes.

I obeyed the prompting and took every opportunity I could to cut my son's toenails. He did not stop me. I cut them slowly, prolonging each opportunity. He did not push me to hurry up.

I constantly sought the help of the Lord in trying to understand what more I could do. The message did not change for a long time. Then another answer came. The Spirit whispered that now there was something additional I could do: I should offer a small hug every Sunday.

Paul's softening did not come all at once. In fact, it took endless weeks and months and years. But it came.

When Paul began to accept my love again, I began to increase my offerings, and he began to accept them.

I am a lot older now. My son is a man.

My lungs don't work very well sometimes. If I am tired, it is hard to hold my arms up and breathe at the same time. One day I was struggling to comb my hair. Paul was visiting at our home. He came into my room and took the comb from my hands and gently and lovingly combed my hair. And in that small act, through his hands he sent love into me.

I shall always be grateful for the answers given me by the Spirit years ago. The answers were real, just as the love is real—and it continues to this day.

And I will soften the hearts of the people.

D&C 105:27

"I DON'T DO WELL WITH KIDS"

PAUL JOHANNSEN

When I was serving as a ward clerk, the bishopric needed to change the ward's Cubmaster. They discussed the matter at length, looking at several different possibilities. They got suggestions from the Cub organization and the Primary president. They prayed for help in understanding whom they should call. Finally they settled on Brother Haskell and asked me to make an appointment for him to come in for an interview. (The executive secretary was out of town.)

I was fairly new in the ward and didn't know Brother Haskell. I called him on Wednesday evening and introduced myself, then said, "Brother Haskell, the bishopric would like to visit with you. Could you come in Sunday at 2:00?"

"Is this about the Cubmaster?" he asked. "Are they going to ask me to be Cubmaster?"

I was surprised that he would ask specifically about the calling of Cubmaster. I didn't even know that anyone was aware that the calling was under discussion. But I answered indirectly, as I had been instructed to do, "I can't really say what this is about, Brother Haskell. They'll tell you when you come in."

What he said next took my breath away. "I can't believe they would call me to be Cubmaster. The bishopric knows I hate the Cub program. They know I don't do well with kids. Why would they even think of calling me to work with the Cubs? Now I'll have to tell the bishopric no to a calling—and I've never done that before—and it's going to hurt my salvation because I wouldn't follow my leaders. But it's their fault because they're the ones making this terrible call to me."

I was stunned at his barrage, and I wasn't sure how to answer.

He continued, "You tell the bishopric I'll come in to their appointment. But you also tell them what I just said."

"I'll relay your message, Brother Haskell," I said.

I told the bishopric what had happened. They were surprised. "We had no idea he felt that way," the bishop said. "Maybe we should reconsider the calling."

On Saturday, Brother Haskell called me back. "Brother Johannsen," he said, "I want to apologize to you."

"What for?" I asked, although I thought I knew.

"When you called the other day, I spoke very much out of turn." His tone was subdued and humble. "When I hung up I told my wife what I'd said, and she said, 'Ron, how could you talk that way? I think you should go pray about it.'

"So I went and prayed about it. I told the Lord how I felt about the Cub program and how I felt about working with kids. I told him it was hard for me and that I was afraid of the idea." He paused, but I wasn't sure what to say, so I just waited. "The Spirit told me I should apologize and that I should accept whatever calling the bishopric asks me to do. Please tell the bishopric I'm sorry and that I'll serve where called."

"Thank you, Brother Haskell," I said. "I'll tell them."

It's true that sometimes it's appropriate for a member to discuss a calling with a leader, and sometimes the leader may feel inspired to withdraw the calling after the discussion. But in this case Brother Haskell had received a witness in advance of the calling that he should accept.

It was a little miracle that happened right there in our ward, our little corner of the kingdom, and it had happened that very week. A man had gone to the Lord in prayer, humbling himself and asking the Lord to help him with his very strong feelings about a calling he feared was coming his way. And the Lord had touched and softened his heart in a dramatic way.

Brother Haskell came to the appointment as arranged. As he somehow had feared, the calling was Cubmaster. He accepted willingly. And then another little miracle happened. He prayed that the Lord would help him with his inadequacies in the calling, that He would help him do well. The result: Brother Haskell was one of the best Cubmasters we had. And he learned to love the boys and the program.

Be strong and of a good courage; be not afraid, neither be thou dismayed: for the Lord thy God is with thee whithersoever thou goest.

JOSHUA 1:9

"WHY DIDN'T HEAVENLY FATHER ANSWER OUR PRAYERS?"

LONI SCHMID

On July 2, 1992, my father-in-law, Earl Schmid, passed away suddenly from a heart attack. My husband, Wayne, got on a flight that same afternoon to hurry to his mother and help prepare for the funeral. The next day I set out on a long-distance drive with our two youngest daughters (Rachelle, then thirteen, and Megan, then five). We had to travel from Vancouver, Washington, down to Rangely, Colorado.

As is our custom, we had a prayer before we left. I asked Heavenly Father to protect us and help us on our way. I knew that the fuel pump on the van was on the verge of going out, but our mechanic said it wasn't necessary to replace it yet. I would have preferred a more reliable car to drive, but I trusted the Lord to help us get there.

We bought some travel games and coloring books and set out on our way. We listened to the radio and sang as we traveled. The day started out bright and sunny, but just outside of Boise, Idaho, we ran into one of the fiercest storms I have ever seen. The sun had gone down, and it became pitch-black outside. The rain came down in sheets, and the wind absolutely howled. The thunder was deafening. We saw several lightning strikes on the sides of the highway. Between the wind and the rain, it became difficult for me to control the van. To make things worse, several huge semitrailers blasted past us, throwing even more water on us and bouncing us all over the freeway lanes. I could barely see through the windshield, but I didn't dare pull over—there was no shoulder on the road, and I was afraid one of the trucks might hit us in the dark. My only hope was to outrun the storm. I gripped the steering wheel for all I was worth to control the van, hoping somehow to get us to safety.

All three of us were terrified. Megan was crying. Then Rachelle began to sing Primary songs. Megan and I quickly joined in. We sang "I Am a Child of God," "Teach Me to Walk in the Light," "I Am a Child of God," "Popcorn Popping on the Apricot Tree," "I Am a Child of God," "Book of Mormon Stories," "I Am a Child of God," and so forth.

After nearly three hours we finally outran the storm. We drove another hour, just to be sure that we had completely distanced ourselves from it. Finally I pulled over at a rest stop. I was shaking so badly I could hardly stand. I thought about stopping somewhere at a motel, but my daughters begged me to keep going until we reached my sister's house in Sandy, Utah, where we had planned to spend the night.

We arrived at my sister's house at 2:00 A.M. I was exhausted, but Elaine had hot cocoa and warm beds for us. I was asleep instantly.

We left the next morning at about 10:30 A.M. It was the Fourth of July and a beautiful summer day. We drove down past Strawberry Reservoir, an unpopulated area. Just as we reached Roosevelt, Utah, the car coughed, choked, and then stopped running. I managed to coast into a gas station. We were only ninety miles from Rangely, but the car wasn't willing to go another foot! I called my mother-in-law's home and talked to my husband's brother Ross. He promised they would leave immediately and should arrive in less than two hours.

When I returned to my girls, Megan nailed me with a question. "Mom, we prayed for protection and that we'd make it to Rangely safely. And now we're stuck here. Why didn't Heavenly Father answer our prayers?" I stood there for a moment, a little stunned, wondering how I could answer without damaging a five-year-old's faith in prayer. Stalling for time, I suggested we get an ice-cream cone at the Dairy Queen across the street, spread our blanket on a nearby grassy spot, and then talk about it.

Once we had our cones and were sitting in a lovely spot, Megan again prompted me with her question. Suddenly the answer was absolutely clear. "Megan," I began, "Heavenly Father *did* answer our prayers, and in more ways than I think we've recognized. Remember that horrible storm in Idaho? What if the fuel pump had gone out during that storm? We would have been drenched or hit by lightning or run over by a truck! What if it had gone out up over Strawberry? We'd have been in the middle of nowhere on the Fourth of July, with no phones anywhere around. We've traveled across Oregon, Idaho, and Utah—most of it far away from any kind of town. When the fuel pump did go out, we coasted into a convenience store that has a bathroom and a telephone. We're across the street from a Dairy Queen. And we're close enough to Rangely that Daddy and Uncle Ross can come to rescue us. We get to sit here in nice weather eating ice-cream cones while we wait. I think Heavenly Father has done a pretty good job of taking care of us. He has answered our prayers."

Megan nodded and seemed to accept the answer.

Wayne and Ross eventually arrived and towed us into Rangely, which is a small town in western Colorado. Wayne's folks lived there almost fifty years. Word travels fast in a small town, and we soon saw how the Lord was answering our prayers for help on our journey in additional ways.

Early the next morning Wayne and Ross were looking over the van, trying to figure out how to fix or replace the fuel pump. As they were tinkering with the van, a longtime family friend, Lowell Levitt, drove up. "I heard your wife had car troubles, Wayne," Lowell said. "Came to see if I could help." Lowell owned several oil field support businesses that employed many people, including a number of mechanics. Wayne and Ross said they thought they could manage, but Lowell just went back to his truck and picked up his car phone. A few moments later he walked back to the two men. "My mechanic will be up here shortly to fix this," he told them. "You have better things to do right now. You go take care of your mama." Relieved and grateful, Wayne and Ross quickly conceded. They found out later that Lowell had sent one of his people on a hundred-mile round trip, on a holiday weekend, to locate the necessary parts.

After the funeral, Lowell let us know the fuel pump had been replaced and that some other work had been done on the van as well. Wayne asked what he owed Lowell. "Nothing," was the response.

"Now, Lowell," started Wayne, "at least let me pay for the parts."

Lowell became misty-eyed. He reminded Wayne that many years before, Earl had been his home teacher. Lowell was inactive, and his wife a nonmember. They had a little boy, a toddler. One day their boy drowned in a small swimming pool. They were out of their minds with grief. Earl visited them constantly, trying to console them. He was gentle and kind. Eventually they started coming to church. Lowell's wife was baptized. In time, they were blessed with other children. Lowell later served in several bishoprics and in the stake presidency. "I wouldn't be the man I am today had it not been for your dad," he said. "He was an answer to our prayers in our time of grief. I can never repay him, but I can help his kids when they are in need. I would consider it an honor and a gift to your father if you'd just let me take care of this. And frankly, I'll be offended if you don't let me." Choked up himself, Wayne agreed.

The truth is that we really did not have the money to fix the car. Lowell was offering a gift and blessing we genuinely needed.

When I heard of Lowell's gift, I went to Megan and Rachelle. I told them of the legacy their grandfather had left and how that legacy had returned to bless us when we needed it. I bore testimony to them that God does indeed answer our prayers. Not only had we been protected on our trip, but now he had provided means for us to get our car fixed so we could return home.

My speech and my preaching was not with enticing words of man's wisdom, but in demonstration of the Spirit and of power.

1 CORINTHIANS 2:4

THAT IS THE WORST LESSON I'VE EVER HEARD!

ALLAN K. BURGESS AND MAX H. MOLGARD

The new missionary district leader could not believe what he was hearing. He was listening to Elder Parker, who had been out for almost two years, stumble his way through the first discussion. Any missionary of worth who had been out three weeks or longer knew the first discussion, but Elder Parker didn't. The early morning study session came to a close, and Elder Parker left with his companion.

The new district leader turned to his companion, shook his head, and said, "That's the worst first discussion I have ever heard. Isn't Elder Parker dedicated enough to learn the discussions?" His companion was surprised that he did not know the discussion; he had always felt that Elder Parker was an excellent missionary.

The next day was their first district meeting of the month, and each of the companionships was to come prepared to share its goals for the new month. It was not an easy mission to baptize in, and the baptism goal of each companionship ranged from three to five people. Then it was Elder Parker's turn to share his baptism goal for the month. When he said they were planning on baptizing twenty people that month, the district leader almost laughed out loud. He thought, *Elder Parker doesn't even know the first discussion but is going to baptize twenty people. This I have to see.*

The next week when the missionaries met, the only elders who had baptized were Elder Parker and his companion. They had baptized five people. The district leader wanted to see how Elder Parker could baptize so many despite his not knowing the discussions, so he asked to go with Elder Parker the next time he was going to teach a first discussion.

The next day, the district leader received a phone call and was invited to go with Elder Parker the following morning to help him teach the first discussion to an interested family. In those days, the discussions were memorized and given almost word for word. Missionaries would take turns, each giving a few paragraphs and shifting back and forth so it seemed like an informal discussion. Elder Parker started the discussion and completely murdered the first part. The district leader took his turn and tried to bring some order back to the flow of the discussion. It was then Elder Parker's turn again—he completely skipped several key paragraphs. By the end of the lesson, the district leader was totally disoriented and confused. He felt that the family probably felt the same way.

When the discussion was over, Elder Parker leaned forward and put his hand on the arm of the family's father. He then looked him straight in the eyes, told him how much he loved him and his family, and bore one of the most humble and powerful testimonies the district leader had ever heard. By the time he finished, every member of the family, including the father, and both elders had tears running down their cheeks. Next Elder Parker taught the father how to pray, and they all knelt down while the father prayed that they might receive testimonies of their own and thanked Heavenly Father for the great love that he felt. Two weeks later the whole family was baptized.

As they were driving away from the discussion, Elder Parker apologized to the district leader. He told him he felt bad that he did not know the discussions better. He said he had always had a problem with memorization. He said he got up at 5:30 instead of 6:00 every morning and spent two hours on the discussions but could never remember them well when it came time to teach. He explained that he knelt in prayer before teaching each family and talked with Heavenly Father about his problem. He would ask Heavenly Father to bless him so that when he bore his testimony, the people would feel his love and the Spirit and know they were being taught the truth.

Humbled, the district leader spent the rest of the day pondering what he had learned about teaching the gospel. For the first time he realized that it was not discussions but love and the Spirit that converted people to the gospel. The district leader never taught the gospel the same way again.

Burgess and Molgard, *Stories That Teach Gospel Principles*, 17–19.

Rejoice with me; for I have found the piece which I had lost.

LUKE 15:9

LOST KEYS

LINDA RIRIE GUNDRY

One day when I was about four years old, I spent a typical afternoon playing with my friend Joyce, whose family lived next door. It was midsummer, and we frolicked outside in the backyard of the duplex where we lived. Our mothers were just inside the open doorways, ironing clothes and making dinner, and they let us play pretty much undisturbed.

When we wandered into Joyce's kitchen for a drink of water, we saw her mother's key ring on the kitchen table. We decided to secretly borrow the keys and play "cars."

We ran outside, the keys jingling first in Joyce's hands, then in mine. We sat in an imaginary car in the middle of the grass. We drove to exciting grown-up places, making car sounds and brandishing the sparkling keys. And then we lost interest and started playing on the rope swing nearby.

The afternoon passed quickly. Our mothers called to us—and with some alarm, we remembered the keys. We had dropped them in the long grass, and we knew we would be in big trouble if we could not find and return them. We searched the yard carefully, calling out, "Just a minute, Mama," and "I'm coming in . . . soon . . ."

We couldn't find the keys no matter how hard we looked. We both started crying. Joyce's mother was sure to be angry. We imagined being spanked or sent to bed early when our parents learned we had lost the treasured keys.

Suddenly a clear picture came into my mind. I remembered a speaker in a recent sacrament meeting, a man who had told a story: A fellow riding a horse was lost in the dark. He dismounted from his horse, knelt, and prayed; and upon opening his eyes after the prayer, he saw a distant light, which he followed to a cottage on the edge of the very village he was seeking. I repeated this story to Joyce and told her we should pray to find the keys. She didn't know how to pray, she said. But I did, and we knelt down in the grass while I said a short prayer.

I said amen, and we opened our eyes. Instantly I saw something glittering in the late afternoon sun. I ran to the spot and found the keys lying half-hidden in the grass. Joyce's eyes lit up, I dried my tears, and we both rejoiced as we anticipated a happy, spanking-free summer evening.

Some thirty years later, my husband, Allen, a social worker, was transferred from Salt Lake City to Arlington, Texas. He and I, along with our five children (later six), came to love the people of Texas. But we hated the searing, humid heat. To make Texas summers bearable, we stretched things financially and built a swimming pool in our backyard, then surrounded it with a high iron fence and a padlocked gate for safety. A stay-at-home mom,

I decided to supplement the family income by teaching swimming lessons to several dozen children.

One summer morning I awoke early so I could begin preparing for the morning's lessons. First I would need to tidy up the pool, and then I would have time to swim a practice lap or two before my little students arrived. But to my chagrin, I discovered that I had lost the key that opened the gate to the pool. Worse yet, it was the *only* key. Someone in our family had lost its twin, and I had foolishly postponed getting a duplicate key made.

I called out to my children, and we all searched the house for the key. We checked every room, looking in likely and then in unlikely places. I was discouraged when I realized I would have to call a locksmith, and my 10:00 class would have to wait, and then my 11:00 class would start late, and so on. I even considered propping up a ladder so we could scale the tall fence, but I realized the impossibility of convincing three- and four-year-olds to climb it. It was hard enough just to coax them into the shallow water!

Finally, a short time before my first students were to arrive, I called off the search, went alone to my bedroom, and prayed fervently that I would be able to find the lost key. I realized, of course, that this was not a life-or-death situation. But I felt certain the key was nearby. I knew that the Lord guides us in even our everyday affairs, and I knew that the Lord knew the location of that key. I expressed these thoughts in my prayer, and after praying, I continued kneeling, waiting for any impressions or ideas that might come to me.

The idea came immediately to my mind that I should look in

the garbage container outside. This had to be pure inspiration, because I would never have thought of it myself. I strongly disliked the idea of hauling smelly things out of the deep container, searching all the way to the bottom, and combing through the week's debris. What if I encountered things even worse than rotting garbage—things like the dead possum we had found in the container one day, or even a scorpion or a huge spider? I'm ashamed to admit that I more or less argued with the Lord. The key was so tiny. The garbage container was so large! But the idea came to me again, clearly and strongly: Look in the garbage container.

I hadn't forgotten the lesson of Joyce and the lost key. So I approached the garbage can and lifted off the lid, dreading the digging, and trusting (albeit rather feebly) that the key was in there somewhere and that I would find it before 10:00.

At the very top of the can, scattered over the bags of trash, was a layer of clean, dry leaves. I brushed aside a few of them, and there was the key to the swimming pool. With a prayer of gratitude, I unlocked the gate and began greeting my tiny students and their parents.

Fifteen years have passed since I taught swimming lessons. We moved back to Utah, and our children grew up, went to the temple, served missions. Most have married, and nine wonderful grandchildren have come into our lives.

I haven't lost any keys for years and years. Recently, I have been praying for some less-tangible things. I have asked for health blessings for myself and my family. Sometimes I have recognized very clear answers to my prayers, and sometimes not. I have asked for blessings for my grown children. Sometimes I have received answers, while at other times I've realized that they need to seek guidance themselves; in such cases, my job is to pray that *they* will be open to the promptings of the Holy Ghost. At times I have prayed for a particular blessing or outcome, only to realize later that the Lord had another plan for me or a family member.

One day several years ago I had the privilege of spending an hour in the office of a member of the Quorum of the Twelve. He told those of us in his office of his own early inclinations toward a particular career, of guidance he received, and of the subsequent changes in his plans. He mentioned some of the great blessings that had come into his life as a result of that guidance and the decisions that stemmed from it. "You know, it wasn't until years later," this Apostle concluded, "that I realized that the Lord had had his hand on my shoulder the whole time."

I believe that, with all my heart. Whether we know it or not, the Lord has his hand on our shoulder at all times. We're being guided, taught, and tutored. Whether we recognize it or not, our prayers are heard and, in the Lord's own time and way, answered. And so I continue praying, both for tangible, earthly blessings and for those intangible blessings that, when they come, may be so quietly bestowed—or so different from what I thought I needed—that it takes me a while, perhaps even a lifetime, to recognize them.

Cry unto God for all thy support.

ALMA 37:36–37

MY BURDEN BEGAN TO LIFT

JOAN BELDON

When I was a mother of three young children, another mother in our ward approached me. She had one four-year-old boy, Justin, who was just a little younger than one of my sons. The mother was a single mom who worked full time. Her day-care arrangements for her son had just fallen through, and she needed someone to watch him. She asked me if I would consider being Justin's full-time, permanent day-care provider. I would have him during work hours five days a week (except for the few hours he went to preschool).

As I listened to her, I could only imagine how it must feel to try to find someone to care for your child. I thought how emotionally trying it must be. I wanted to help her.

At the same time, I already had three small children. While I was blessed to be able to stay home to care for them, I felt that I was always pushed to the limit. I didn't feel that I had any extra time or energy to spend on anything else, especially another child. We could certainly use the money she would pay us for watching him. But I knew that if I agreed to care for him, it couldn't be for the money. I would want to do it to help her and to help Justin.

I told Justin's mom that I would talk to my husband and get back to her. We talked it over and then went to the Lord in prayer. After our prayers, we clearly felt we should tell her yes. Justin's mom was thankful and relieved to have a good place to send her son.

But having Justin at our home soon felt very burdensome. Sometimes he was a lot of trouble, especially in the first several months. Sometimes he was very well-behaved. But I just felt that an extra child every day was too much for me to handle. In my heart I hoped that the situation would change so I wouldn't end up watching him very long.

I pondered my feelings. Why did I feel so negatively about caring for Justin? My husband and I really had no doubt that it was the right thing to do. I also knew that serving with an unwilling heart was not as pleasing to Heavenly Father. Yes, taking care of my own children was tiring and difficult at times. Yes, being a mother was definitely a burden. But I didn't *feel* burdened with my own children.

As I thought about it further, I realized that I didn't feel burdened by my own children because I loved them so much that I didn't focus on the burden of taking care of them. I loved them so much that taking care of them was a joy. I knew I loved Justin just as I try to love all of God's children. But the Spirit bore witness that if I could love Justin as I love my own children, taking care of him would not *feel* like such a burden.

So I prayed for help, asking Heavenly Father to help me love Justin as I loved my own children. Then I waited to feel differently. Nothing happened. I asked again for him to help me. Then I waited, expecting a change. The change didn't come. I didn't know why, but I still felt overwhelmingly burdened.

So I went back to my Father in Heaven with a more fervent prayer. I asked him to help me know if there was more I needed to learn about this problem or if there was something I needed to work through more. The Spirit helped me to know that there was.

Through prayer and pondering and exploring my feelings with the Spirit, I learned that I was blocking feelings of love from forming with Justin because of fear. What if I loved him more deeply and then his mom decided at some point to send him to another day care? What if I loved him and he didn't remember me when he grew up? What if I loved him and then had to send him home to his mom every night and weekend and day off? I was afraid of the pain I would feel if I loved him and then lost him.

When I understood this roadblock to my receiving this love, I prayed some more. I asked Heavenly Father to help me not to worry about the pain. I asked him to help me be open to the love. I asked him to help me be willing to feel the pain so I could feel the love. I asked him to change my heart.

Then the miraculous change started to take place. My feeling of burden began to lift. It was still hard in many ways, but I felt a peace about it. My heart was opened to let Justin in. Then I started to miss Justin if his mother had a few days off. I started to be interested in how he did at preschool. I felt more love for him. I started hoping that he could keep coming to my house for a long time.

I did end up caring for Justin for a long time. After a while we felt like he was a part of our family, and he felt like he belonged. As time went on, I became convinced that being a day-care provider for Justin was not only a blessing for Justin and his mom, but it greatly blessed my family and me as well.

I am so thankful that Heavenly Father helped me understand my heart and then gave me the gift to change it.

Ye shall know the truth, and the truth shall make you free.

JOHN 8:32

"THE FAULT LIES WITH YOU"

TRUDY HUGHES

My husband and I loved each other very much, but we had never learned to communicate without periodic arguments. (We do much better now—the years have schooled and mellowed us.) One day we were having another of our arguments. At this point I can't remember the subject of contention, but I can still remember the feelings. They were very intense. Although such arguments were a recurring pattern in our home, I hated them. They would often get loud, and I hated the fact that he always had to be right. My chest hurt, and I was feeling hysterical. Why couldn't he see that sometimes I was right?

I ran to the bedroom, fell to my knees, and began calling upon my Heavenly Father. I was weeping and praying that I would feel peace in my soul. I felt miserable. I feared that things would never be right between me and my husband. And I was thoroughly frustrated that he couldn't give more place to my opinions.

As I prayed, I heard a soft, manly voice whisper to me, "My

daughter, in this thing you are in the wrong. The fault lies with you."

I was amazed to receive that message from the Spirit. I had been so convinced of my position, so positive. But as I reflected on the message, I could see its truthfulness. And the truth gave me great peace and even gratitude, even though I was the one who was in error.

I got up off my knees and went back into the other room, where my husband was. One look at his face and I could see that he was feeling as miserable as I had been. "I'm sorry," I said, giving him a hug. "The mistake was mine. Please forgive me." And he did, freely and fully.

I am so grateful that our Heavenly Father loves us so much that he will reveal to us such little things as this, even tiny nuances of our feelings, so that we can improve our relations with others and grow to be more like him.

They did fear their God and did supplicate him for protection.

3 NEPHI 4:10

PROTECTING OUR "BRONZE BOMB"

WAYNE DONALDSON

During the academic year of 1987–88 I was a doctoral student at the Hebrew University of Jerusalem, the Mount Scopus campus, located in northeast Jerusalem. My wife, Camille, and our four children (we've since had two more) accompanied me to the Holy Land. Our first goal was to establish a modest household that would satisfy our basic needs for a twelve-month period. We leased a two-bedroom apartment in a village about ten miles north of Jerusalem. Through the help of Church members who were then living in Jerusalem, we acquired used furniture, bedding, pots and pans, dishes, and other items.

We also purchased a vehicle. Since we were living on a student's budget, we shopped around for the best bargain, finally deciding on an older sedan that was just large enough for our family. This vehicle had been imported from Cyprus, an island in the Mediterranean, to Haifa, a port city in northern Israel. Over the years, the once-red car had experienced fading, and certain areas of the body had corroded. The resulting color was bronze, almost rust colored. As a joke, one of our friends labeled it "the bronze bomb," a name that stuck.

Notwithstanding its imperfections, the car served us well. The engine was reliable, and the car's interior was acceptable. We felt that it was a small miracle that we had such a marvelous means of transportation in a land that once primarily used camels and donkeys. We took our bronze bomb shopping, especially to purchase groceries and other necessities. Occasionally, we took it on a family field trip to explore various regions of the Holy Land. We drove it when making visits to friends. But most significantly, it transported us to church every Sabbath without fail. In the Holy Land, Israel's Jewish population kept the Sabbath sacred by shutting down the public transportation system. Our car was therefore definitely a necessity. Without it we would have been somewhat immobile, and we would have lacked the means to travel to church, a journey of ten miles in one direction. We loved that old car, and we were thankful to our Father in Heaven that it served us so well for the entire twelve months that we resided in the Holy Land.

In our family and individual prayers, we continually prayed for safety while living in the Holy Land. We also prayed that our vehicle would continue to function properly.

It was my habit to drive the bronze bomb at an early hour from our home to the Hebrew University of Jerusalem. I arrived early every day to obtain a coveted parking space to the south of campus. Since I was one of the first to arrive, I was able to park in the same parking stall every day (almost without exception) for several months. Only rarely did another driver arrive early enough to park in my favorite place. Day after day, month after month, I parked in this same place.

One day was different, however. I offered my normal prayer for protection before I left for school. I arrived early enough to park in "my place," and once again it was available. But for some reason I felt I should park elsewhere. So I did. I drove to another place, parked and locked my car, and left it there for the day.

Late that afternoon, after attending classes and completing my schoolwork, I left the university complex to return to my car. Acting through habit, I walked to the place where I normally parked. As I exited the building and looked where my car was customarily parked, I saw another car in its spot. But this car was not whole; it had been destroyed during the day. The car in my spot had been fire-bombed by a revolutionary or activist and had been entirely burned up.

Had my own car been parked in its usual spot, it almost certainly would have been destroyed. My family and I would have been immobilized and unable to attend church every Sabbath. We would have been unable to partake of the sacrament and fellowship with other Church members. But Heavenly Father had heard and answered our numerous prayers for safety and protection, which had been offered for so many months.

I can only hope that the owner of the vehicle that did get demolished was able to quickly and easily replace it with another.

I have no greater joy than to hear that my children walk in truth.

3 JOHN 1:4

"PRAY FOR HER"

ANITA R. CANFIELD

I had to fly to Mexico City one Thursday evening to inspect a project site under my design direction. The clients were leaving on Saturday for a two-month tour of their factories in Europe and the Orient, and there were dozens of questions to be resolved with them and the contractors that Friday. It had been a last-minute request on their part, and my trip was going to be an overnight but very intense visit.

I arrived at the hotel around midnight and went immediately to sleep. Around 3:00 in the morning, I was awakened by an excruciating, stabbing pain in my mouth with what would be classified as an extreme dental emergency.

My husband had done some dental work on me earlier in the week in preparation for further work the next week. I was in excruciating pain. I didn't know what to do. A million dollars' worth of decisions was resting on me the next day. I had to be clearminded and alert, especially with the language barrier; my Spanish is only adequate and requires great concentration on my part.

My first thought was to call my husband and get the name of a drug that would stop the pain. Then I worried that it wouldn't be the same dosage or type in Mexico. Then I wondered if the concierge would be able to find someone at 3:00 in the morning to even obtain it. And then, with complete realization, it occurred to me that any drug strong enough to knock out this pain would completely knock me out, and I would be useless the next day. I didn't know what to do.

Then came the distinct and clear message: "You have faith. You know what to do."

I climbed out of bed, knelt in prayer, and told the Lord of my situation and all that concerned me, and I asked him to please take away the pain long enough for me to complete my work the next day. Before I said "in the name of Jesus Christ, amen," the pain vanished. Instantly, in a moment, it was gone. I thanked him and went back to sleep.

The next day I was able to answer the questions, make urgent and very critical decisions, and finish on time to catch my flight home. By the time I was in customs in Los Angeles, the pain was returning. When I landed in Las Vegas several hours later, I had another full-blown dental emergency!

But that is not the whole story. Two days later was fast Sunday. In our monthly family testimony meeting, I told of my experience and my witness of the power of faith and prayer.

My fifteen-year-old son grew amazed. I could see his countenance change. When I finished speaking he asked, "Mom, was this Thursday night?"

"Yes," I said.

"And was it about 2:00 in the morning?"

I thought about that. It was 3:00 in Mexico, but with the hour time change, I told him it was 2:00 in Las Vegas.

Suddenly he was filled with emotion and told me the beginning of the story. He had been awakened at 2:00 in the morning that night with a voice that said, "Your mother is in trouble; pray for her." He had slipped out of bed, and on his knees, with real intent, had said, "Heavenly Father, my mom has faith. Tell her what to do."

The Lord heard his prayer and reminded his mother of her faith and that she knew what to do.

Canfield, *Remember and Perish Not*, 74–75.

Blessed are all they who do hunger and thirst after righteousness, for they shall be filled with the Holy Ghost.

3 NEPHI 12:6

"MY LIFE HAS NEW DEPTH AND JOY"

MARY W. FORSYTHE

When I was nineteen the young men my age had the chance to go on missions. When they returned it seemed like they had had a jump start in spiritual learning and experience that had not been available to me. I felt a little slighted, for I deeply desired spiritual growth.

I continued faithful, marrying in the temple and becoming a mother to several small children. Although I served in both my home and the Church, my opportunity for significant spiritual growth seemed small and my true desire for it seemed largely unsatisfied.

Eventually, my husband was called to be the bishop. Some of the feelings I had had in my youth returned. I realized that my husband was on an upward spiral of opportunity for spiritual growth. Meanwhile, I knew my role was to be in the home. The children would need me, and my responsibilities there would be greater than ever.

I wanted my husband to be blessed in every way, but I

wondered how I, in my limited opportunity, could also obtain the spiritual gifts and blessings that were available.

I began to voice my feelings in prayer. I struggled to understand how I could receive spiritual strength in my circumstance. I pleaded to know how to fill the hunger I felt inside.

At length I learned a most basic and vital truth: One's spiritual growth is a personal matter between each individual and Heavenly Father. It is not related to Church calling or outward opportunity. The chances to grow are available to everyone, and if we will desire and seek with a true and honest heart, the way will be opened. Knowing this, I was then able to bow down and seek guidance in understanding how to obtain gifts and blessings of the Spirit.

When the sought-for inspiration came, I felt fearful and weak. The Lord seemed to be telling me that to grow in things of the Spirit, I must learn to recognize, obtain, and live with the gift of the Holy Ghost. I knew this was possible. I had heard stories of those who had the Spirit in their lives. But I never felt like I was very good at it. I expressed in prayer that I had always felt weakness in this area and I asked to know how one such as I could live so that this gift would be a greater part of my life.

During one fervent prayer my mind recalled a scripture, but I did not know where it was to be found. I turned to the Topical Guide, looking for the word "weakness," and found the scripture that had been renewed to me: "If men come unto me I will show unto them their weakness. I give unto men weakness that they may be humble; and my grace is sufficient for all men that humble themselves before me; for if they humble themselves before me, and have faith in me, then will I make weak things become strong unto them" (Ether 12:27).

I read and reread this passage. I certainly felt humble and weak. I wondered if I had enough faith to allow my Father to make my weakness into my strength. I desired and prayed for that kind of faith. With a hope in my heart, I began to ask for the help I needed to obtain the workings of the Spirit in my life.

In the space of time that my husband served as bishop a miracle occurred in me. As I continued to seek for guidance and as I submitted increasingly to the promptings I felt were from the Spirit, I began to be changed. Every opportunity and experience I needed for spiritual growth were given to me.

Heavenly Father helped me to know the things I could do. I gained confidence in my prayers and in the answers that came. My faith expanded, and I gained an unmistakable testimony that the Savior's grace is sufficient for all, even for me. If the desire is there, if my heart is right, and if I do all that I can, then, through the atonement of Christ, my weaknesses are made into my strengths.

Now I can tell my own stories about the gift of the Holy Ghost. I can bear sure witness of the workings of the Spirit. I can testify concerning the blessings available through the Atonement. I feel that these things are surely strengths in me.

It does not matter where or when we serve. It matters only that we have faith in our Savior Jesus Christ, that we believe in the blessings promised by a loving Father, and that we seek his help in obtaining them. My life has new depth and joy. My gratitude knows no bounds.

Blessed be God, even the Father of our Lord Jesus Christ, the Father of mercies, and the God of all comfort; who comforteth us in all our tribulation.

2 CORINTHIANS 1:3–4

COMFORT FROM THE FOG

RUTH DEBRY

Through repeated pregnancies and childbirths, my mother's health deteriorated, and the doctors told her she would never be able to have children again. Yet seven years after having five girls and a boy, she had a miracle baby, a special gift from God, her last son.

After the birth of my baby brother, following medical advice, my mother had a hysterectomy. Her health greatly improved. She was a loving mother to all seven of her children throughout her entire life.

Years passed. After having five children of my own, I was faced with the identical quandary. Should I try to restore my anemic body back to health through the same surgery? I prayed repeatedly, both by myself and with my husband. But I remained uncertain. It was such a huge decision. It would mean I would have no more children. Was that Heavenly Father's will? I didn't know.

By this time my mother was sixty-eight years old. Her health had again declined. She suffered from Parkinson's disease, which robs loved ones of their former selves. She also experienced dementia and most days did not even recognize me as her own daughter.

One day I walked out of the doctor's office with troubling news that I would have to make an immediate decision. I stopped at my mother's rest home and sat on the edge of her bed. I was frightened and confused and poured my heart out to this beautiful, kind woman who had given me birth. I didn't expect a response. Her mind wouldn't allow one. I just needed to talk.

Suddenly she sat up in her bed. For a brief moment in time, her glazed eyes focused on mine, and she said, "Ruth, you need to get this operation so you won't be anemic and sickly all the time." Astonishment showed in my eyes, and I hugged my mother tightly as tears of thankfulness escaped from my eyes. Then she faded once again into her own confused world, and I was left clinging to the human shell that had once housed my mother.

I sensed the Spirit so powerfully at that time, I knew that my Heavenly Father had answered my prayer. He had permitted my mother to give me comfort and a confirmation that all would be well with my decision.

Thou heardest the voice of my
supplications when I cried unto thee. . . .
For the Lord preserveth the faithful.

PSALM 31:22–23

A SECOND CHANCE

LOIS L. SAUNDERS

I was returning from Relief Society one evening back in the days when it was held during the week. The cold Alaskan winter had been broken by a warm spell, bringing rain that had turned the snow-packed side roads into treacherous sheets of ice. The main roads were mushy or bare but not dangerous.

As I approached our side road, a voice said, "Don't turn in. Use the other road."

I pushed the thought aside. It was strange for me to think such a cowardly thing. Some used the other road in bad weather to avoid the steep hill, but I never had. I'd always made it over that hill, and always on the first try. I turned and began the steep climb. I prided myself on the fact that I knew how to get the car moving at just the right speed to make it up.

I was almost to the top when my wheels began to spin. I realized then that it had not been my fears telling me to go around, but the still small voice trying to warn me. I would have to back down and go around.

When I put the car in reverse, it began to slip sideways toward the steep twenty-foot embankment. The experience quickly turned into a nightmare as nothing I did seemed to change the car's course. The car refused to be controlled, and I kept sliding dangerously near the edge. Wrestling with the car, I silently prayed for help—and the car stopped.

I offered a prayer of thanks and put the emergency brake on, but it would not hold. Each time I lifted my foot from the brake pedal, the car slid a little more toward the edge. I again prayed for help. Nothing happened. I honked the horn, hoping someone would come to my rescue, but there was no response.

I realized I was too upset to hear an answer to my prayers, so I prayed again, asking this time that I would be calm and that I might be able to hear the answer to my desperate request. I immediately became calm. My heart no longer felt as if it were trying to escape my chest.

I told Heavenly Father that I knew he could pick up that car and set it down safely if he wanted to. I pleaded with him to guide me to do what I must to save myself and the car. When I had finished my prayer, I remained sitting with my eyes closed, waiting for an answer.

I saw in my mind's eye that if I turned the steering wheel one way I would go off the road, but that it would hold if I turned it the other way, which I did. Then, as though someone were sitting in the backseat, I heard a voice tell me to ease my foot off the brake. I did, and the emergency brake held.

The voice then told me to get out of the car. I obeyed, but as soon as my feet touched the ice, I began to slide under the car. As I reached out to touch the car for support to keep from falling, the voice seemed almost to shout as it commanded me not to touch the car. I pulled my hand back as if the car were red hot. Because I couldn't stand up on the ice in my shoes, I removed them, and my warm stockinged feet kept me from sliding. I could see that the back wheel of the car was about six inches from the edge of the embankment.

I crossed the road and put on my shoes, then walked in the snow to the bottom of the hill. At the nearest house, I phoned my husband.

As I returned to the road, I heard a noise up the hill. I was horrified to see my car slipping down the hill. "Don't worry," said the voice, "It's under control." I could see that the car had turned from the edge and was backing down the center of the road, as if someone were driving it.

Just past where I stood, the car moved to the left side of the road and came to a gentle stop, one rear wheel in midair, the other resting on the gravel shoulder.

As I stood marveling at the miracle I had just seen, my husband came walking over the top of the hill. I explained what had happened, and we bowed our heads in thanks for my protection. My husband then got in the car and didn't even stir the gravel as he drove it from the shoulder onto the road.

Years later, the road over the hill was straightened—cut down to a less hazardous climb—but seldom did I use it, especially in winter, without thinking of the day I learned a vital lesson about the importance of recognizing and obeying the promptings of the Spirit.

Saunders, "A Second Chance," *Ensign*, Mar. 1987, 32.

In the strength of the Lord thou canst do all things.

ALMA 20:4

HE BLESSED ME IN MY FEELINGS

JAMES ALLEN WILKINSON

I had been serving as Gospel Doctrine teacher for three years—and was loving it—when the bishop invited me and my wife into his office. "I have prayed carefully about it," he said, "and I feel that the Lord would be pleased if you were my new executive secretary."

All my life I've been taught to say yes to callings, so I said yes. But even though I said yes, I felt unsure about the rightness of the calling. I went home and knelt in prayer, asking the Lord if that calling was indeed his will. The Spirit whispered a quiet but definite *yes*.

But in the days that followed, I struggled with the idea.

"You've never been able to keep a day planner," my thoughts said. "You think you can keep the bishop's schedule?"

"You can't even organize your own office. Now you think you can organize the offices of the ward?"

"You know how calling people on the telephone sometimes makes you uncomfortable. Now you're going to be calling people all the time."

"And what about all the extra time you're going to be spending in meetings? You're already stretched to the limit."

I went back to the Lord again, asking anew if it was his will that I accept this calling. Again the answer was a clear *yes*.

And still the negative thoughts continued. I didn't know if those negative feelings were my own doubts and fears or if I was getting interference from the adversary.

One day I read this statement from President Gordon B. Hinckley:

"Is there a missionary who has never felt fear? I know of none. Of course we feel fear now and again. Some are fearful of tracting. Some are fearful of their own capacity. Some are fearful of dogs. Some are fearful of speaking out in declaration of the truth. All of us experience fear now and again. But God has not given us the spirit of fear. That comes from the adversary. When we recognize that, then we can tell the adversary to get behind us, and we can go forward with courage" (*Teachings of Gordon B. Hinckley*, 221).

I knew he wasn't just talking to missionaries; he was talking to all of us who struggle with callings in the Church.

Whether my feelings were from my own weaknesses or were augmented by the whisperings of the adversary, I had finally had enough. I prayed fervently and repeatedly for peace, for reassurance, for clarity and consistency in my feelings. The Lord heard me, and he answered. Every time those thoughts and feelings resurfaced, I asked for help, and every time I asked for help he granted it, helping me to know that whatever my inabilities, he would magnify me in this calling, he would support and sustain me, and he would enable me to accomplish his will in it.

It took awhile for me to be comfortable in my new calling, but the comfort level came, and I was able to serve the bishop (and the Lord) well—not because of my own ability, but because of his help. I am ever grateful that he loves me and helps me even in the small and invisible areas of life, like my fleeting or all-too-persistent feelings.

Whatsoever thing persuadeth men to do good is of me.

ETHER 4:12

LEARNING TO LISTEN

RHONDA MCNEIL

My thirst for knowledge was insatiable. A convert to the Church, I felt I had a lot to learn, and so I read all the materials I could get my hands on. Yet, after ten years, I still did not comprehend how people received revelation. The burning sensation and that still small voice others talked about seemed to elude me.

Marriage only added to my frustration. When decisions had to be made, it was my husband who always got the answers. His track record was terrific; we had the help we needed when we needed it. I found it easier to pray that *we* would get the answer, then just follow his counsel.

Still, every once in a while, my inability to receive revelation would leave me with a nagging, let-down feeling. This usually came when I went visiting teaching. I would kneel in prayer and ask that the Lord help us discern the needs of those sisters my companion and I were to visit. Then we would make our rounds. The sisters never seemed to need our help, and so I would let things drift, all the while yearning to be of inspired help.

An employment change for my husband brought us into a

new city and a new ward. I was so bothered by my previous "failure" as a visiting teacher that I did all I could to avoid the Relief Society presidency. But in spite of my best efforts, it didn't take them long to find me and make the call. My initial visits with the wonderful women my companion and I were assigned to promised to be only the first in a series of special visits. I worked hard on the lessons, trying to bring special meaning to them for the sisters. I wanted to give them all that I could. Yet, when I prayed to know the needs of these sisters, the heavens were silent.

One morning while I was dusting, a thought came into my mind—call Amanda. I quickly pushed it away so I could get on with my work, but while I was sorting laundry, it returned. I impatiently told myself that Amanda was busy preparing her cooking mini-lesson for homemaking meeting that evening. She wouldn't have time to chat. I went on to the dishes, but once again the thought came—call Amanda. I gave up, dried my hands, and went to the phone. All the time I was dialing, I was practicing my apology for bothering her when she was so busy.

When Amanda answered the phone, I found myself not apologizing but asking if she needed help with her cooking lesson. To my surprise, I found that she had been on her knees in prayer asking for help. She needed someone to fry extra portions of the food so that each sister attending homemaking meeting might have a taste. Out of desperation, she had almost decided to skip that part of her demonstration.

A couple of weeks later, I was writing letters to some of my relatives when I was troubled by another thought. Whenever I would pause in my writing to think, the names of the three sisters on my visiting teaching route came into my mind. I pushed the thought aside and kept on writing. But the more I pushed, the more it persisted. Finally, I let it stay just to see what would happen. A few minutes later I was busily engaged in writing short notes to the three sisters, telling them simply that I was thinking of them and wishing them a happy day.

With the pressures of everyday activity, I easily tucked this experience in the back of my mind. One day, my daughters and I got involved in making and decorating a batch of sugar cookies. It turned out to be a very *large* batch of cookies. I knew we could never eat all of them. Again, a thought came into my mind—the sisters on my route. I had learned by this time not to ignore those kinds of thoughts, so the girls and I quickly wrapped the cookies and went to deliver them. On the way back home, my oldest daughter said that sharing the cookies had been a great idea; it had made her feel good.

After I put the girls to bed, my daughter's comment returned to my mind. I suddenly realized that these thoughts that popped into my mind were a bit unusual. I cornered my husband that night and asked him to tell me what was happening. He explained that the thoughts were just my way of getting the answers I had sought for so long. Each had shown me a way to help my sisters.

The more I thought about this, the more I realized I had been limiting myself by expecting to receive a constant flow of revelation on behalf of my sisters. Sometimes all a person needs is a friendly face when the day is dragging. None of us face major problems all the time, nor do we always need outside help in dealing with them. More important, I found that I *could* receive inspiration. But it would come according to the Lord's will, not mine, and in the way he tailors for me. I felt as though a load had been lifted from my shoulders.

With my new understanding came renewed gratitude for the wisdom of my Heavenly Father. I knelt to thank him, and to ask for help in remaining worthy of his Spirit in the future.

McNeil, "Learning to Listen," *Ensign*, Apr. 1986, 45.

Out of small things proceedeth that which is great.

D&C 64:33

THE LOGICAL CHOICE

LISA MANGUM

Summer was drawing to a close, and the scent of fall was in the air. I was going to be a sophomore, and I was a little nervous to make the leap to high school. But first came the all-important school schedule. I sat on my bed with all my elective choices spread out around me. I could take psychology instead of P.E. if I wanted to. I didn't have to take home economics ever again. I could sign up to work on the school's literary magazine. The freedom was heady.

I dutifully filled in the required classes: intermediate algebra, driver's education, English, and history. Add in seminary. I was left with two elective classes. Creative writing was an obvious choice since I dreamed of someday being a professional writer. One space left—one hour of time at school that I could spend however I wished. The logical choice was to take another year of German. I was college-bound, and I knew I needed two years of a language to qualify. I had started to write down the class code when another elective class caught my eye: beginning drama.

I knew that my best friend, LeeAnne, was going to take a

drama class since she dreamed of someday being a professional actress. If I took drama with her, it would guarantee that we would have at least one class together. Tempting. I paused, leaning back against my headboard.

Wait. Take drama? Was I crazy? I had panic attacks during the Young Women's sacrament meeting program at church. No, German was the logical choice.

But still . . . I'd known LeeAnne since the fourth grade. Was I willing to risk high school without her?

I could tell this would take some serious thought. High school was a major turning point in your life; everyone said so. I wanted to make sure I was doing the right thing, so I decided to pray about it. But I knew I couldn't just expect a voice from heaven telling me to take drama or to take German. I knew one way answers come is to study it out in your mind, make a decision, and then ask if it is right. So I did what I am best at: I made a chart.

I created a column for both drama and German, listing the pros and cons under each. Drama had only one pro: "Class with LeeAnne." It had three cons: "I'm shy and scared to speak in public." "I've never acted before." "It won't help me get into college."

In contrast, German had three pros: "I've already had a year of German." "I like the language and the culture." "I'll have a head start on college credit."

Try as I might, I couldn't think of any "cons" to the idea of taking German. After all, I reasoned, I might still have English or history with LeeAnne.

So it was decided. German. I bowed my head and prayed. I explained my situation, reviewed my choices, and then indicated that I was choosing to take German. Was that the right choice?

I guess I was expecting a resounding *yes*, so I was rather startled to discover I wasn't feeling anything at all. How odd. I prayed again. *Did I mention I was going to take* German*?* Nothing.

It couldn't mean I was supposed to take drama, could it?

I modified my chart by adding a few more "pros" to the drama column: *Maybe I'll overcome my fear of public speaking. Maybe I'll discover a hidden talent.*

If the Lord was going to throw me a spiritual curveball, then I was prepared to take another swing at it.

So it was decided. Drama. I bowed my head and prayed. I explained my situation, reviewed my choices, and then indicated that I was choosing to take drama. Was that the right choice?

Almost immediately and somewhat involuntarily, my lips twitched up into a smile. I looked down at my chart again. A grin spread across my face. Could it be? My insides felt feather-light. I could have sworn my skin was glowing. I ran to my parent's room. "I'm taking drama!" I declared and proceeded to tell them the whole story.

But the story doesn't end there. I did in fact have drama with LeeAnne. And I did overcome my shyness, which was a blessing because the next year I was hired at a bookstore where I interacted with strangers all day long. In addition, the money I earned from my job helped pay for college. And I did discover I had a hidden talent for drama, not a great talent, but I was confident enough to take drama for the next two years of school.

Being involved in drama for the three years I was in high school was truly a blessing, as it provided me with a social circle that I might not otherwise have had. Maybe the German Club would have been intellectually stimulating, but I doubt they had as much fun as we did in drama. My journals and photo albums are filled with our adventures and plays.

And it was in the advanced drama class that the greatest unexpected blessing came into my life. It was in that class that I became friends with a fabulous young man who introduced me to new music, new books, and new ideas, who valued my opinion, who studied with me, who ate lunch with me, and who kept me sane more times than I can count—a young man who eventually became my husband.

I have never regretted filling in that last elective space with drama. It was, after all, the only logical choice.

I will not leave you comfortless.

JOHN 14:18

A NEWLYWED ADVENTURE

RICHARD PETERSON

In 1961, just two months after I got married, the National Guard unit I was in was activated by President Kennedy in the so-called "Berlin Crisis." Premier Khrushchev and President Kennedy were facing each other down at the height of the Cold War, and that dispute meant I had to leave my bride in Salt Lake City and go on active duty at Fort Leonard Wood, Missouri. The separation was painful for me and my wife, and we prayed that it would be short. We were relieved and grateful when, after only two months of initial combat training, I was allowed to send for her, and we set up housekeeping just outside the little town of Rolla, Missouri, located about twenty-five miles from the army post.

Before JoAnn arrived, again in answer to prayer, I was excited to be able to find a place to rent, a small cottage located on a farm just a mile from town. Our landlord, Mr. Coffman, ran a cattle operation he called "Green Acres Farm," where he had converted a concrete milk house into a little cottage, consisting of a living room, bedroom, kitchen, and bathroom. He said we could rent it for $50 a month if we would pay the propane heating bill in the winter.

The farm itself lived up to its name. Mr. and Mrs. Coffman lived in a lovely, white mansion, complete with pillars holding up a porch roof over a broad veranda. The house was situated on a tree-shaded knoll overlooking the pastures and fields, which were divided from each other by honeysuckle hedges and where herds of black Angus cattle grazed. Two large, white barns with green roofs dominated the farm complex, and in the distance was a forest of oak trees growing on a ridge that marked the boundary of Mr. Coffman's holdings. With the fragrance of honeysuckle flowers in the air and evening displays of fireflies dancing in the darkness outside our windows, the tiny cottage was an idyllic place for a couple of newlyweds to live.

We enjoyed our first Thanksgiving and Christmas together, with a few army friends around us, but far from our families in Salt Lake City.

My assignment on the army post was to work as an orderly in the post hospital, and my shifts alternated from day to night, as the duty roster required.

A month or so into the new year, after working an all-night shift, I drove home from the post early one morning to find JoAnn lying on the couch in the living room. She had been dreadfully ill during the night, throwing up and hemorrhaging, and she was so weak she couldn't raise herself to a sitting position. She was ashen white and could barely hold her head up. She told me she thought she needed to go to the hospital.

I carried her to our car, a Volkswagen beetle of an early design, and drove frantically the mile or so into Rolla to the hospital there. After an initial evaluation, JoAnn was admitted and taken immediately into emergency surgery.

After an hour or so, which I spent nervously pacing, worrying, and praying, a doctor came to find me and reported that JoAnn had experienced a "tubular pregnancy," which he explained was a somewhat common occurrence where a fertilized egg attaches itself to the wall of one of the fallopian tubes instead of to the inside of the uterus. As the embryo had grown, it had eventually ruptured the tiny tube, which had caused her internal bleeding. He told me he had repaired the damage but added that my wife would lose the function of that one fallopian tube. She would also have to remain in the hospital a few days. He suggested I go home, rest, and come back after she had recovered from the anesthetic.

The doctor said JoAnn's condition was a relatively "common occurrence." Perhaps it was to him, but it certainly wasn't to me. Numb with exhaustion and literally sick with worry, I drove back to our cottage. We were each only twenty-two years old—kids really—and our parents and families were two thousand miles away. I had only vaguely understood the condition the doctor had described, and though he had assured me that JoAnn was going to be fine, I had seen how sick she was, and I wasn't certain I wouldn't lose her. I also feared that we might not be able to have children in the future.

With those thoughts running through my mind, and feeling

totally alone, I knelt by our bed and offered the most earnest and emotional prayer of my life, pleading with the Lord for my wife's recovery and asking that we would eventually be able to have children.

After praying for I don't know how long, I began to feel a warm, peaceful feeling wash over me. I heard no voice, but I received a calm and unmistakable assurance that all would be well. My fear went away.

It wasn't long until JoAnn was sufficiently recovered to come "home" to our little cottage. She soon regained her normal health and strength, and we enjoyed the rest of the extended honeymoon we had been provided by the U.S. government. Then, with the political crisis ended, we returned in August to Salt Lake City to take up our schooling and work.

The Lord's comforting answer to my prayer sustained me in that awful moment of doubt and fear—and my prayer was further answered over the next few years as we went on to have five wonderful children.

And the Lord said unto Joshua, This day I will begin to magnify thee.

JOSHUA 3:7

"I EXPECTED INSTANT RESULTS"

N. LYNNE ALLRED

Once I was called to be the ward Relief Society president in an area where visiting teaching was in the thirtieth percentile. I pledged to the Lord that we would try to reach 100 percent of the sisters, and I began to pray fervently for the Lord's help. A key element of those prayers was to discover whom the Lord wanted as my visiting teaching leader.

One day I sat talking with a sister from another ward about visiting teaching. Her name was Robyn, and she confessed that she was an awful visiting teacher, saying it was her partner who dragged her out each month, made the calls, and always brought some thoughtful thing for each sister. But she said that by being dragged out each month, she was beginning to enjoy it. As I listened to her, I recognized the whisperings of the Spirit in my soul: I should call this sister to be my new visiting teaching leader!

Robyn's background certainly didn't seem to qualify her to be a leader. She had run with the wrong crowd for much of her life, had been on drugs, and had a history of immorality. She also struggled daily to stay mentally healthy. Yet she had confessed her sins and repented, leaving them behind, and had returned to full fellowship in the Church. Nevertheless, I received the strongest impression that the Lord wanted her to be called to that position. How could that be possible? She didn't even live in my ward! At the end of the conversation she told me she would soon be moving into an apartment in our ward. There was my answer.

The day Robyn accepted the position, I bore my testimony to her that I *knew* she had been called by the Lord. My testimony was so strong that I expected instant results. I saw none—none at all. During the first few months I couldn't even get her to call the district leaders to get the statistics. I ended up calling them myself. One month, determined to get her to function, I called her every day for seventeen days until she finally followed through and called those four district leaders! I began to wonder if I should release her. What puzzled me was the strong spiritual impression I had had to call her. I knew it had been an answer to prayer, and I was really bewildered that she wasn't functioning. I prayed and asked the Lord for additional guidance. I prayed with all my heart for him to bless her with a testimony of visiting teaching and to teach her of her true worth in his kingdom.

At church the following day I had a meeting with Robyn. We sat at a table in the cultural hall, and I again bore testimony of the inspiration I had received about her calling. I told her I had never felt stronger about any other calling I had prayed about! Robyn, in tears, bore her testimony to me that she also knew she was the right person, and she committed to perform the calling. I felt the Lord's Spirit and knew he was in charge. Amazing things began to happen.

The Spirit whispered that Robyn should help me to visit the sisters on our new-move-in list. Robyn had confessed to me that she and many other sisters were timid about visiting sisters they did not know. We visited many houses in the pouring rain that day. Most were in an area of town that women avoided at night.

We visited the home of Angel Lauber. She was very happy to see us and invited us into her home. I gave her the visiting teaching message on "Gaining a Testimony of the Restored Gospel" and then felt prompted to add a message on "How to Perfect Yourself." Angel began to weep. She was deeply touched by the message. She tearfully related an unusual experience to us.

Angel worked at a nursing home as an LPN. She had worked two shifts back to back and was very tired. Toward the end of her day she had an experience that suggested she needed to get her life in order. She knew that one day she would be required to stand before the Savior and make an accounting of her life. And she knew that if she didn't feel comfortable doing it now, she wouldn't feel comfortable then, either. She had a strong impression that she needed to analyze her life and come up with a plan whereby she could *perfect* herself. The experience and the feelings weighed heavily upon Angel's mind.

As she was preparing the evening meal, she kept thinking about her feelings. She knew she didn't know how to come to perfection. She decided to pray about it as she blessed the food. She poured out her soul to God and begged him to send her someone who could show her what she needed to do. When she looked up from her prayer, she saw Robyn and me coming up the walk. She listened quietly to the message about gaining a testimony of the restored gospel, but as I started talking about how to perfect yourself, she could no longer contain herself. She wept openly.

We visited all ten homes on our list that night. Every home was a spiritual feast along the very same vein—all ten! Oh, the joy we felt! We were gone for six hours (from 2:30 to 8:30)! We were frozen, wet, and muddy, but our hearts were full as we drove home that evening. Robyn's face radiated joy. I knew the Lord had prepared experiences like this to strengthen her testimony of visiting and home teaching.

As we neared the entrance to our subdivision, Robyn suddenly said, "Lynne, I know we have been gone from our families a long time, but I feel that we need to visit one more person before we go home tonight." After a day like that, I wasn't about to start arguing with the Spirit! I asked, "Who?" She replied that the missionaries had given her the name of a new convert, Alice, who lived with an abusive, alcoholic, crack-addicted boyfriend.

"If you feel impressed to go, then we had better do it right now," I said. When we entered Alice's home a few minutes later, we learned that a nonmember neighbor named Suzy was also there. It soon became apparent that these two women had lived very hard lives. Four-letter words peppered their speech. But we also discovered that they were both at a crossroads in their lives. We talked with them awhile. Or rather, I should say Robyn did, for she quickly formed a tight bond with these sisters. She spoke with power given from the Holy Ghost. She had also suffered from an abusive relationship, and she counseled Alice on how to escape her situation. I could see that Robyn was reaching Alice.

It was getting late, and we got up to leave. But before we did, Suzy asked if she could attend church with us. Then her husband stopped by, and he expressed the same desire.

Words cannot express the feelings that were in our hearts that night. I felt so privileged to have been able to witness the love that Heavenly Father feels for each of his children. He knows their hearts, desires, and needs.

That night Robyn gained a powerful testimony of the importance of visiting Heavenly Father's children in their homes. She had felt the powerful spirit that attended us all night. From that moment forward, she entreated the Lord to help her share her testimony of visiting teaching with others. She prayed for inspiration in her calling as a visiting teaching leader, praying with all her might. I personally witnessed the answers to those prayers, for Robyn's testimony transferred into every phone call she made and every conversation she had about visiting teaching. Through love, she was able to share her new vision of visiting teaching with every partnership. No heart could deny the powerful witness that she bore! Two months later the ward achieved 100 percent visiting teaching.

Prayer. Prayer began it all. Prayer led me to Robyn. Prayer helped Robyn to fulfill with true excellence the calling the Lord had given her.

On that cold, rainy day I was taught by the Lord. The world may pass us by without giving us a second thought, but the Lord looks at our heart and knows our potential. He knew the pearl of great price that lay within Robyn. He knew that she was the key to visiting teaching in that area. And she was.

I was an hungred, and ye gave me meat: I was thirsty, and ye gave me drink: I was a stranger, and ye took me in.

MATTHEW 25:35

STRANGERS IN THE NIGHT

ATWELL J. PARRY

My wife, Elaine, is from the San Francisco Bay area. When we got married we moved up to Idaho to start our family, but at least once a year we would take our children back to California to see their grandparents. We would travel at night because we didn't have air conditioning in those days and because the little ones would sleep most of the way.

We traveled across the Idaho, Oregon, and Nevada deserts to Winnemucca, Nevada; then we turned west and drove to Alameda, the city where Elaine's parents lived. For many hours the towns were few and far between, usually sixty to seventy-five miles apart. The roads were all two-lane blacktops—there were no freeways. It was beautiful desert country with nothing but miles of road and a few jackrabbits. We always started with a humble prayer asking for safety, protection, and help on our journey.

One year we loaded our three little kids in the car and headed for California. All went well for a few hundred miles; then our right front tire blew out. By the time I was able to stop the car, the front rim was ruined. I put the spare tire on, and with the Lord's blessings we had an uneventful trip the rest of the way.

While in Alameda, I went with Elaine's father to find a replacement for our ruined rim. We went to a wrecking yard, and I gave him the model, year, and make of my car. After checking the specifications, the salesman sold me a wheel. I bought a new tire to put on it, and we were all set for the trip back.

After spending a wonderful week in Alameda, we headed back home to Idaho. We left at about six in the evening.

The hours passed. The car was running well, the kids were asleep in the backseat, and we were making good time across the Nevada desert. Then halfway between Lovelock and Winnemucca (a distance of some thirty-five to forty miles each way), our right rear tire went flat. It was about five minutes after midnight. I pulled to the side of the road, took the new wheel and tire out of the trunk, jacked up the car, and removed the flat tire. I told Elaine it would only be a moment, and it was. The new rim would not fit on my car. The holes in the wheel were about a quarter of an inch off from the lug bolts on the car.

I looked up and down the highway; there was not a light anywhere in any direction. The road was absolutely deserted. We prayed that someone would come by—and that they would stop. No one came. We prayed some more, and we waited. Finally, after about a half hour, we saw headlights coming toward us from Winnemucca. They were going in the opposite direction from where we wanted to go. The car slowed down, then passed us, then turned around and pulled up beside us. A well-dressed black man got out of his car and asked if we were in trouble.

At this point, the civil rights movement in America was in its early stages; there was often an uneasy truce between blacks and whites. But on that dark road in Nevada, there seemed to be no races, just two men, one in trouble and the other offering help.

I explained our problem. The man invited me to put the tire in his trunk and offered to take me to Winnemucca. (Everything in Lovelock would have been closed by that hour.) I hesitated because it would take him in the wrong direction. He responded that he had plenty of time and that he didn't have to be in San Francisco until later the next day. Then he turned to his wife and asked her, "Would you mind staying with this lady so she won't be alone out here in the dark with her children?"

This kind stranger went out of his way to take me to Winnemucca to have my tire fixed. It was a round trip of more than seventy miles. All of this time his wife, another beautiful stranger from out of the night, sat with my wife to keep her company. Elaine told me later that the woman was concerned and friendly and very easy to talk to.

When we returned, the man waited to see that the tire was on the car. I offered to give him money to fill his car with gas, but he wouldn't hear of it.

As our good Samaritan drove away, I put our car in gear and started off again. We went about ten feet when I stopped and announced to Elaine that we had another flat tire. It was unbelievable. We still didn't have a spare that worked. I got the tire off, and we then renewed our prayers. We thanked our Father in Heaven for helping us earlier and asked him to bless us that someone else would come by—someone who would stop and help us. After a while, another vehicle came by. This time it was a fellow in a pickup. He stopped and asked if he could help. We threw the flat tire into the back of his pickup, and he drove me to Winnemucca, dropping me off at the same service station I had used before. The same man who had fixed the first flat tire was still on shift and helped me again. Then I went back out to the highway to flag down a ride back to the car and my stranded family. A third kind stranger was happy to help me. When I reached my family, we said one more prayer—this one of gratitude for kind strangers and answered prayers, as well as asking for continued help—and then went on our way.

It was about 8:00 in the morning when we finally arrived in Winnemucca. My wife and children had spent eight hours waiting while I made two round trips to Winnemucca, a total distance of some 150 miles.

I'm sure the Lord has a special place for such caring people, "strangers in the night," who went out of their way to help a family in trouble.

A man that hath friends must shew himself friendly: and there is a friend that sticketh closer than a brother.

PROVERBS 18:24

BEING A FRIEND FIRST

ARDETH G. KAPP

Years ago when I had just turned seventeen, I left my small hometown of Glenwood, Alberta, Canada, which has a population of approximately three hundred people. I went away for my senior year of high school because the courses I needed for graduation were not available to me at home. I knew only one person in my new school, and I was scared. I hadn't had any experience in making friends except with those kids I had grown up with. I didn't wear the latest fashions like the other girls, so I looked different. I wasn't a part of the in-group or of any group, for that matter. I was away from home, homesick, and lonesome. Even if they had asked me, I didn't have the money to do the things the other kids did. I yearned for friends. There was so much talking going on, it seemed that everyone else had lots of friends. *How do you get in?* I wondered. No one was discourteous, but I felt ignored, as if they didn't know I was there.

Can you imagine how desperately I wanted friends, or at least one friend? I remember feeling alone, a long way from home.

Kneeling by my bed day after day, night and morning, I prayed for friends, I pleaded for friends. I wanted boyfriends, girlfriends, young and older friends, member and nonmember friends. I felt I needed friends for my survival. I talked to my Father in Heaven and promised that in every way I would strive to do what was right no matter what, if I could just be helped to know how to make friends in my new situation. The thought came to my mind that maybe there were others who felt as I did; maybe I should try to forget about myself and be a friend first. I thought, *I can smile, and I can say hi.*

I believe that thought was a whispering of the Spirit in answer to my prayer. I began to focus on being a friend instead of having a friend. I listened to the Spirit. I did smile, and I said hi to everyone. I learned to be friendly. At first it was hard, but before long it became easier. At the end of my senior year, I was nominated by the student body as the representative girl for the high school where I had attended only one year. Some may have considered it a popularity victory, but I'll always know it was in answer to the fervent prayer of a sixteen-year-old who learned how to be friends with everybody.

Kapp, "Being Friends with Those Who Are Not Latter-day Saints," in Randal A. Wright, *Friends Forever*, 106–7.

I would that ye should remember, and always retain in remembrance, the greatness of God, . . . and his goodness . . . towards you.

MOSIAH 4:11

A GENEROUS EMPLOYER

KEVIN STOKER

As they walked along a New England country road in the mid-1940s, Elders Truman Madsen and Reuel J. Bawden wondered where they would get their next meal.

The missionaries "were rather unpopular among these farm folk," writes Elder Madsen of the experience. The two missionaries had spent the night sleeping in a barn and hadn't eaten in twenty-four hours. So they left the road and entered a grove of trees to pray for help in getting something to eat.

"This happened often in our country work—going off into the woods to pray," writes Elder Madsen. "It wasn't a habit—it was a necessity. Who but the Lord could help us in these hostile country areas? We were without purse or scrip. But he in whose work we were engaged was ever within reach, the unfailing source."

In prayer, Elder Bawden pleaded, "Father, wilt thou open the way for us to have a bite to eat."

As they arose, the elders saw a trout jump and strike a fly in the small brook flowing through the grove of trees.

"Oh, for a fishing pole!" Elder Madsen muttered.

"What's wrong with what you have in your hands?" queried Elder Bawden.

The tattered umbrella didn't look like much, but it was all they had. Elder Bawden doubled up some thread and attached a doctored safety pin to the end while his companion located a worm. Elder Madsen then gave the contraption a try.

Dangling the line over the grassy bank, he thought, "Can this be the way the Lord is going to answer our prayer . . . , or do I just have a flair for the unusual?"

He already knew the answer. The Lord had answered their prayers before, so there was no reason why he couldn't arrange for a fish to bite.

Wham! A trout struck hard. Elder Madsen jerked, and a fish flew over his head, off the hook, and onto the bank. As they looked for more worms, tears filled their eyes.

They caught and cooked six fish, offering heartfelt thanks to the Lord before eating them, fins and all.

"You know," said Elder Bawden as he picked up his suitcase, "the Lord is a mighty generous employer."

Stoker, *Missionary Moments*, 23–24.

The Lord seeth not as man seeth; for man looketh on the outward appearance, but the Lord looketh on the heart.

1 SAMUEL 16:7

BRAD AND ME

ELISABETH JOHNSON

From the time my son Brad was old enough to express an opinion, I could tell that he had an edgy temperament. As a baby he was quick to cry—more so than any of my other children. At the age of two, he began to throw himself on the floor and kick and cry if he didn't get what he wanted.

As Brad got a little older, his temper seemed to become a more serious problem. As a four-year-old, when he was upset he would get mad, yell, hit people, or throw toys. When he got started in such behavior, it was often difficult to get him to calm down. I would end up in his room with him for up to twenty minutes, sitting with my back to the door to keep it closed while he cried, yelled, screamed, and struggled to get the door open. Sometimes he would then get mad at me and try to hurt me. My husband was a great help if he was home, but these episodes usually happened when he was gone. I felt that most of the problem rested on me alone.

I knew firsthand how detrimental a bad temper can become

if it is allowed to grow. My own father had brought much sorrow to our family through his temper. I felt like I had to teach Brad to not give in to it. I could not allow him to grow up and feel like blowing up was O.K. I wanted to turn his behaviors around now, before they became very bad habits.

When Brad was not upset he was a very kind, loving, and tender boy. He was always good at giving us hugs and was often gentle and loving to his siblings.

As I prayed repeatedly for help with Brad, I received an understanding about my son. Through the whisperings of the Spirit, I understood that Brad was not behaving as he was because he was a bad person or because he was filled with anger or hate. Heavenly Father told me that Brad was a good boy—a choice spirit with much light and love in him. But Brad had this one weakness that was his trial to overcome.

One of the first things I prayed about was to learn what punishments would be appropriate and best for Brad. The Spirit helped me understand that I couldn't discipline Brad in the same way as I did my other children because Brad was not the same as them. I couldn't just read a self-help book. I learned that the best thing for me to do was to ask in prayer how I should deal with each child—especially Brad.

As I prayed further, I felt it would be useful to use the idea of "time out"—shutting him in his room alone for a few minutes when he misbehaved. But that only made him more angry and the situation worse. I wondered if I had misunderstood the Spirit's direction. But as I asked further, I learned two nuances: I should use "time out" if Brad was trying to hurt someone or if he was uncontrollable. Second, if I used "time out" I needed to stay in the room with him. This worked better.

I prayed about many different punishments and, in the end, didn't feel good about any of them. But I did feel good about making a "good mark paper" for Brad. We taped this paper to his bedroom door. Every day that Brad went through the whole day without hitting anyone, he got one "mark" on his paper. Every night I praised him for his good mark or talked to him about why he didn't get one and asked him to try to do better the next day. It took quite a few months, but he really got better at not hitting when he was mad. I was so thankful to learn this one thing that would help him.

But I learned an important lesson as I continued to work on the problem in prayer: more important than the punishments was how I reacted to Brad's behavior. I knew that many times I did not react to his anger in the best way. I would get very frustrated with him. Sometimes I would react to his yelling and anger with yelling and anger. It took a lot of strength to go to the Lord and ask him how *I* could do better. It was scary for me to ask him what mistakes *I* had made and what *I* was doing wrong. He told me to not concentrate as much on my actions or reactions as on my feelings. If I could learn to *feel* the right way in hard situations, then right actions and reactions would follow.

So I prayed and pondered and tried to remember how I felt when Brad was acting up. I came to realize that in those bad situations I felt despair. I felt helpless to change Brad. I felt that nothing I said or did made any difference. I felt alone.

It took me a long time to learn the right way to feel and then to feel it. I prayed a lot. I asked Heavenly Father to help me come to the right feelings. I tried to tell myself, "Feel hope, feel hope, feel hope" when I was in a tense, angry situation, but I was still struggling.

As I worked on these things, I started to get frustrated with myself. I loved my children so much, and I wanted so much to do the best for them. I had a few bad days in a row, followed by a night of praying and crying. I pleaded with Heavenly Father to help me feel the right way when dealing with Brad. I pleaded for an answer. Then Heavenly Father taught me. I needed to learn that I was not alone in my problem. Brad was Heavenly Father's son first, and our Father loved him and was with me in parenting him, helping me do the right thing. Alone, I was not enough to handle this. But with God and me together, we were strong enough, good enough, patient enough, and sufficiently full of hope that Brad and I could both change.

With the Lord's help, things began to get better. When I felt the right way, I really did react in a much better way. I would talk to Brad calmly and just try to love him until his upset feelings were gone. Sometimes I could distract him from his anger by talking to him about other things (stories of Jesus, funny things, tickling him, or telling him things that I liked about him). I would ask him to calm down and tell him I knew he could do it.

I would hold him when he would let me, sing to him, and just love him.

And it didn't matter how angry he had gotten, how much he had yelled, or how long it took him to calm down, when he did calm down I would say, "Brad, do you know what you just did that was so great?" He would say, "What?" Then I would say, "You calmed down! You did a great job! You are so great! Give me five!" Then he would smile and give me five and a hug. With the guidance and help of the Lord, I was able to stay calm and do the right things to help Brad.

While neither of us is perfect in these things, we are both doing much better. I am so grateful for all the answers Heavenly Father has blessed me with during these trying years. Because of his help, I truly know that my Heavenly Father is a partner with me in caring for my children.

It is not requisite that a man should run faster than he has strength. And again, it is expedient that he should be diligent.

MOSIAH 4:27

LIGHTENING MY DAILY BURDENS

LILLI TAYLOR

Between my fourth and fifth babies, I began to experience a number of physical problems, including a fair amount of fatigue. I thought my fatigue wouldn't last long, but I was wrong. It went on and on for years. My doctor did many tests and could find nothing wrong.

It was very discouraging; I soon had five children to take care of, and I wanted to be a good mother to them. Caring for five children can take a lot of time and energy. I wanted them to have clean clothes, nutritious meals, a clean home. In addition, I wanted to be faithful as a Latter-day Saint. I knew I needed to be a good friend to others, to love and serve them. I desired to magnify my calling and support my husband in his calling and his career. I wanted to be supportive of my children's schools and of activities in the community. Many ward activities deserved my support and attendance: temple night, Relief Society homemaking (enrichment) night, ward parties, Primary activities, Scouts. I wanted to be a good person, a righteous member of God's church, but I felt despair when I thought of all the things I was supposed to be doing. I also felt stressed because the doctor could find nothing wrong with me. I couldn't help thinking, Am I just lazy? Why can't I feel like I've had enough rest? How can I feel so bad and the doctor can't explain it?

I often felt guilty for not doing all the things I was supposed to be doing. I have a testimony of the truthfulness of the gospel. I know we are led by a true prophet; but because of my energy level, I was having a real struggle in trying to live the gospel and the prophet's counsel. I prayed and prayed that Heavenly Father would help me feel more energetic and less tired. But the blessing I sought didn't come, so I tried with all my heart to feel that he knew what was best even if I didn't understand.

I heard talks in church and read scriptures counseling me to turn my burdens over to the Lord. I wanted to do that—but how? How could I turn this particular problem over to the Lord? I prayed for Heavenly Father to help me turn my burdens over to him. Gradually I began to understand how this blessing could be mine.

For me, the answer was to ask for guidance on many more things. At first I was apologetic. I didn't want to bother Heavenly Father about some of the little things in my life. But the Spirit encouraged me to proceed, and I knew it was right and good. The key seemed to be to ask Heavenly Father to help me set my priorities. What should I spend my time on, what activities I should go to, how much I should focus on keeping the house clean? Was I sleeping too much?

Sometimes the answer to these questions was not what I wanted to hear. Sometimes the whisperings of the Spirit suggested that I not do something I really wanted to do. Sometimes the Lord asked me to do something I would have preferred not to do. It was a struggle sometimes to obey the feelings I received when I asked for help with priorities. I prayed for help to feel a desire to do his will and not mine. I found that as I sacrificed for the Lord and strove to do his will, he blessed me with the energy I needed to accomplish what he would have me accomplish. Other times I felt distressed that my home needed cleaning and organizing but the Lord instructed me to not work on it at that time. As I followed his instructions and prayed for help, he blessed me to bear my dirty house without feeling it as a burden. These small miracles built up my testimony and my faith in God.

In this way I was able to turn my burden over to the Lord. I sometimes received criticism from people for not doing the things the way they thought I should. This was hard for me, and I prayed for help not to worry about what other people think but to rely on what Heavenly Father thinks. I was truly blessed as I tried to do what Heavenly Father would have me do.

As I proceeded down this path, I came to wonderful feelings of peace because I knew Heavenly Father knew me and my limitations; he knew what was best for me to focus on at any given time. Because I was receiving guidance from the Spirit, I knew my priorities were correct. The more I turned my life over to the Lord and tried to be his servant, the more he sustained me.

I still can't do everything everyone wants me to do, but I can do everything Heavenly Father wants me to do in a given day. Of course, I'm far from perfect in it, but this process has saved my life—and has taught me how to gradually, step by step, become all that God would have me be. It has shown me how to avoid running faster than I have strength and, while doing so, how to continue to be faithful (see Mosiah 4:27).

Their preservation was astonishing . . . , yea, that they should be spared. . . . And we do justly ascribe it to the miraculous power of God.

ALMA 57:26

"UNSINKABLE"

TOM HEWITSON

In 1978, Patrick, a young Nigerian man and captain of a supply ship for Her Majesty's Royal Navy, was about to greet his cab, which was waiting in the street outside of his flat in East London. He grabbed his leather satchel and rushed out the door, only to be met by two missionaries from The Church of Jesus Christ of Latter-day Saints. He paused only long enough to receive a Book of Mormon from them, then boarded his cab. "That was a close one," he thought, feeling he had barely "escaped" a meeting with missionaries. He shoved the book into his satchel without a second thought, had the cab take him to the dockyard, and was soon on his ship and bound for the Indian Ocean.

At that same time, I was a typical teen growing up on the west side of Salt Lake City, contemplating life after high school graduation. Even though I had been baptized and held the priesthood, I wasn't really raised in a religious environment. My knowledge of the gospel of Jesus Christ was somewhat limited.

That year, President Spencer W. Kimball announced that the

Lord had revealed that all worthy males in the Church could receive the priesthood. Television and newspapers were abuzz with the story. Since many of my friends were African-American, it had a strong impact on me, even though I wasn't fully aware of what "the full blessings of the priesthood" meant.

Time passed, and my life took a positive course. I began prayerfully seeking guidance, pondering about serving a mission. As I read the scriptures and studied the gospel, I was continually reminded of President Kimball's revelation. I had a strong feeling that when I received my mission call, I would be going somewhere like Zimbabwe or Johannesburg, South Africa, where I would serve among my African brothers and sisters. Then the call came. England London East Mission? "Of course," was my quiet, consoling answer.

Several months and zero baptisms later, I was assigned to a new "greenie"; together we served the people of East London. Impatience grew into discouragement, and we repeatedly fell to our knees in fasting and prayer, seeking help in finding those who would accept our message. We spent many hours talking with our Heavenly Father and many more hours diligently working. Through it all, I never forgot my feelings about President Kimball's revelation.

Then one Sunday at church, I looked out the glass doors of the foyer to the sidewalk on the street. A young African man stood there looking at me, holding a battered Book of Mormon in his hand. I moved to greet him at the door, where I shook his hand. "My name is Patrick," he said, "and I'm here to join your church."

My companion and I spent the next week almost living at Patrick's flat—teaching him the discussions, bearing testimony, laughing, crying, and praying. As we got to know Patrick, I suddenly understood why President Kimball's revelation had meant so much to me. Patrick was a "golden" investigator in the classic sense. He never questioned a single principle, and he seemed to know the Book of Mormon inside and out. I baptized him, and my companion confirmed him the following Saturday. We rejoiced that our Heavenly Father had heard and answered our prayers.

Why did Patrick's conversion take two years, from the brief encounter with the missionaries in 1978 to his baptism in October 1980? That is another story of prayer.

In his thick Nigerian accent, Patrick told us the story. When he was met by the missionaries, he shoved the Book of Mormon into his satchel and forgot about it, then set off with his crew on a three-week training assignment. Several days into the mission, while Patrick was sailing off the southern tip of India, modern-day pirates besieged his vessel. They swiftly killed everyone aboard (they thought) and threw them and most of their belongings into the sea. Although badly wounded, Patrick managed to cling to life. He tearfully told of how his leather satchel with the Book of Mormon in it was the only thing keeping him afloat. "It was unsinkable!" he cried. He described how he, along with the bodies of friends, bobbed up and down for hours, and how he prayed to live—then when night came, in desperation he prayed that he would die before the sun rose.

The sound of a diesel engine woke him up the following morning. While in and out of consciousness, he watched while several Indian fishermen rummaged through the debris and bodies. They found him alive, pulled him aboard, and took him to the nearest coastal village. There they left him with a local family who cared for him and nursed him back to health.

His only belongings were his life-saving leather satchel, containing a soggy Book of Mormon, and his military orders. Months passed before Patrick was able to walk. He spent most of his time reading, taking Moroni's promise to heart, praying to know "if these things are . . . true." He truly grew to love the family who had unselfishly taken him in.

Almost eighteen months passed before Patrick was able to make contact with the British Embassy. Then the news began to spread throughout Britain about his survival experience. I vaguely remembered hearing something about it, but I never supposed his story of prayer would intersect with mine.

It was a beautiful day in the fall of 1980 when I had the pleasure of meeting Patrick, just three weeks after he had returned to England. The Book of Mormon he held in his hand was in tatters. The light in his eyes was glorious. The power of prayer had led each of us on a wonderful journey, a journey of discovery and truth. He told me that he was going back home to Nigeria to teach his people the gospel.

It has been years since I have communicated with Patrick, but I still pray for him—and I have no doubt he still prays for me.

I will impart unto you of my Spirit, which shall enlighten your mind.

D&C 11:13

PRAYER BEHIND A SURGICAL MASK

DANIEL L. ORR II

As an oral and maxillofacial surgeon I've seen more than my share of miracles. I recall a patient submerged underwater for thirty minutes who completely recovered after a tracheotomy and other procedures. Earlier this year, a young lady scheduled for five hours of trauma surgery left the operating room in less than an hour after she'd received a priesthood blessing. However, I believe that all things denote God's hand (see Alma 30:44). I'm simply blessed to be in a profession in which I'm daily privileged to see and appreciate the hand of God in surgical matters. After all, no matter what we do as surgeons, our procedures are extremely low-tech compared to what our Father in Heaven does.

From time to time I am also blessed with an immediate answer to a prayer in my heart. Such answers are real, direct, and filled with light.

Once I had a patient who was undergoing an elective surgical procedure that involved removal of diseased tissue. The patient was under general anesthesia and was therefore unconscious. The procedure was expected to take ten or fifteen minutes. But during the procedure, which is one I've completed thousands of times without incident, a complication occurred. Hard dental tissue that should have been removed was instead, inadvertently, displaced into a deep anatomical space filled with delicate vessels and nerves. The procedure immediately changed from routine to one where an extreme amount of technical expertise was required.

Over a period of an hour, I made a number of attempts to retrieve the lost tissue, but I failed again and again. The professional literature describes what to do in such a case, calling for an additional major surgical procedure that is time-consuming, debilitating, and fraught with potential additional complications. I did not look forward to the additional surgery, and I knew my patient would not want it either.

I was totally frustrated and disappointed in myself. I had been practicing oral and maxillofacial surgery for more than twenty years and had taught my specialty on the university level. But I could see no other option than to put my patient through the trauma of the additional major surgery.

Before moving from the first procedure to the more invasive operation, I stopped for a moment, closed my eyes, bowed my head, and offered a prayer to my Father in Heaven. It is possible that others in the room knew I was praying, but I did not announce my actions, and my face was covered with a surgical mask. At any rate, when I'd finished asking my Father in Heaven to help me with this patient, according to his will, I opened my eyes and took a long, deep breath. Literally within seconds the thought of how to rectify the complication came to my mind. I had a sense of disbelief that so simple a solution could have been overlooked, both by me and by the many other professionals who had dealt with a similar problem. I turned back to the patient and followed through on the idea the Spirit had given me. I was able to correct the complication and successfully complete the procedure within a matter of minutes. I then gratefully watched my patient quickly and fully recover from the incident as though nothing extraordinary had happened.

Later that week I was talking to another surgeon who, by coincidence, was preparing to take his patient to surgery for the same complication I had experienced with my patient. My colleague was planning an aggressive procedure similar to what I had been contemplating, and he asked me to assist him. When I mentioned my experience (without the prayer), he was excited, saying the idea was brilliant. We agreed to use the new technique on his patient; if it didn't work we would fall back to the original surgical plan. We were gratified to come to the same positive result, and in short order.

My colleague suggested I publish the new technique in the professional literature as a technical advance, which I did. (My description of the procedure was published as "A Technique for the Recovery of a Third Molar from the Infratemporal Fossa: Case Report," *Journal of Oral and Maxillofacial Surgery* 57 [Dec. 1999], 1459–61.) After the article's publication, I received several sincere thank-you calls from surgeons around the country. In my dealings with my professional colleagues, I have not always acknowledged my Heavenly Father's hand guiding mine (D&C 59:21), but his help was certainly there, an immediate and very real answer to a brief prayer uttered behind a surgical mask.

Keep my commandments, and assist to bring forth my work, . . . and you shall be blessed.

D&C 11:9

BLESSED WITH STRENGTH

SARAH ANN EADS

Being a wife and mother have always been my top priority. I love the role of mother, and when my children were growing up I always remained at home to care for and train them, sometimes at a sacrifice of worldly goods and comforts. When I wasn't serving my family, there was always plenty that needed to be done in service in the ward and stake.

At one point when I still had several children at home, I was offered a prestigious position with a successful company. This position would give me a chance to make a real difference in the lives of those with whom I would work. The salary would be high.

On a trial basis I participated in some training sessions. I found that I related well with others and could even be instrumental in helping some of them change their lives for the better.

I fasted and prayed for inspiration. For three weeks I struggled. I asked my Heavenly Father again and again to help me understand what I should do.

While I was still in this process, my bishop invited me in for an interview and called me to serve as the ward Relief Society president. Now my decision was much more difficult. I could not fill all the roles that were before me. I further fasted and prayed and asked for Heavenly Father's help.

During personal scripture study one day, I read Doctrine and Covenants 11:8–10:

"Verily, verily, I say unto you, even as you desire of me so it shall be done unto you; and, if you desire, you shall be the means of doing much good in this generation.

"Say nothing but repentance unto this generation. Keep my commandments, and assist to bring forth my work, according to my commandments, and you shall be blessed.

"Behold, thou hast a gift, or thou shalt have a gift if thou wilt desire of me in faith, with an honest heart, believing in the power of Jesus Christ, or in my power which speaketh unto thee."

As I read, the Holy Ghost bore witness to my soul that this was the answer to my prayer. Worldly position meant nothing compared to the work of the Lord. The Spirit also indicated that the blessings of doing the Lord's will far outweighed any earthly salary I might receive. The scripture also contained a promise to me (as to all of us)—the Lord would bless me with the spiritual capacity I needed to do his work.

I knew those whose lives I could best touch were those of my own family and those of my ward sisters.

I felt the warm love of my Father in Heaven when I accepted

the position as ward Relief Society president. As I fulfilled the calling, I was blessed with strength in my role as wife and mother.

Through this experience, and others, I have gained an undeniable testimony of the power of prayer and inspiration that can guide us in our times of need.

In every thing by prayer and supplication with thanksgiving let your requests be made known unto God.

PHILIPPIANS 4:6

CHARLIE

EILEEN D. TELFORD

He was only sixty-eight, but he looked much older. His emaciated body lay strapped to a narrow hospital bed. His breathing was shallow; his vital signs were failing. This was Charlie, one of twenty patients in the medical-surgical ward at State Hospital (a mental institution).

"How's he doing, doctor?" I asked the resident physician who was struggling to find a vein in the man's flaccid arms.

He shook his head. "Charlie's dying. It can't be long."

"Do you think he'll go tonight?"

He shrugged. "It could be a couple of hours—or a couple of days. It's hard to say."

I nodded. I understood, but I didn't like it. As the night nurse, I'd have to decide whether or not to call his family.

In a normal situation at a general hospital, I wouldn't have hesitated to call the family, but here at State things were different. Charlie, like most of the patients, had been hospitalized for a number of years. Families had learned to live and function without them. Many had given up caring. I liked to believe that most of the families would want to be present at the time of death. But calling them in the middle of the night without being certain that death was imminent was against hospital policy.

And I *didn't* know when Charlie would die. Neither did the doctor or the evening shift nurses. Medically, it was impossible to determine how soon death would come—only that it was en route.

I stood at Charlie's bedside, pondering. I tried to imagine him differently—no longer aged beyond his years and bereft of physical health and mental faculties including memory, but younger, a husband with a happy wife and laughing children. I had the feeling that if I were one of them, I would want to be present at the time of his death to somehow let him know that I still cared, that I still loved him.

I was filled with compassion for Charlie and his wife. They still loved each other, I was sure. They would want to be together at the time of his passing—but I stood between them because I didn't know when that would be.

In the past when I have been confronted with problems I could not resolve, I turned to a constant source of help: prayer. I turned once again to that source, bowing my head and praying aloud that I might know if I should call his wife or not.

Words came forcefully to my mind and heart: I should contact her right away; he would be called home before daybreak. I no longer wondered what to do. I knew that Charlie had less than six hours to live and that it would take his wife an hour to get there.

Immediately I phoned her, explained that Charlie's condition had worsened, and suggested that she come in. To my surprise, she was reluctant.

"I have a workshop to attend tomorrow," she explained, "and I need to sleep."

"But his condition is worsening," I emphasized. "It might be a good idea if you were here."

"What good would it do?" she agonized. "He hasn't recognized me in months. It's hard to see him this way." She sighed heavily. "All right," she said, softening, "I'll come in. I'll be there between 7:00 and 8:00 in the morning."

But that would be too late! Frantically, I searched for words. "I think you should come in sooner than that!" I said. "Like right away!"

"Why?" she asked.

I wanted to tell her what I'd heard in answer to prayer but could not. "Ma'am," I began slowly, "your husband is dying, and I think it would be a good idea for you to come in soon." I paused. "But that decision is up to you."

"Then I'll come in first thing in the morning," she replied, and hung up.

I was disappointed in her decision, but I knew that it was hers to make. I tried not to think about it as I checked the other patients, but silently I prayed that she'd change her mind. Fifteen minutes later she called back.

"Do you really think he's dying?" she asked.

"Yes," I replied.

"Do you think he'll die before morning?"

I paused briefly before answering. "Medically speaking, I can't say for sure. But my feeling is that he will die before morning."

"Then I'll come in," she said. "I'll be there in an hour."

I was elated about her change of mind, but as I thought about it, I became concerned. How sad it was that her dying husband wouldn't be able to recognize her or realize the effort she was making to be with him.

I went about my duties, pondering the situation. At 1:00 A.M. I distributed medications, and as I walked down the silent corridor I again felt the need to pray. So, going to a linen closet where I could be alone, I once again asked our Father in Heaven for help—that Charlie would at least be able to recognize his wife, that this one last time there might be love between them, if not in words then at least in tenderness and shared feelings.

It was 3:00 A.M. when she arrived. I was surprised at her youthful appearance. Her salt-and-pepper hair was neatly styled; she was slim and petite. She looked a youthful fifty, while Charlie looked an ancient eighty. She introduced me to a lovely young woman who had come with her—her daughter.

I walked with them to Charlie's room—partially to make them comfortable and check on Charlie but mostly to see if my prayer had ascended above the top shelf of the linen closet. As they went to his bedside, a light seemed to pass through Charlie's vacant blue eyes. His clenched fists relaxed, and he tried to speak.

His wife sat in the chair beside him, gently stroking his arm. Then Charlie smiled.

"I think he recognizes me!" she cried. There were tears in her eyes. And in Charlie's. And in mine.

"I know he does," I answered, and quietly left the room.

Periodically I checked Charlie's vital signs. They were slowly worsening, but Charlie continued to be calm and gentle—contrary to his usual erratic behavior. He was receptive to his wife's touch and soft-spoken words of love. He did not speak, but they communicated; love flowed between them.

At 5:00 A.M. Charlie was still maintaining. Sunrise was less than forty-five minutes away; I began to worry about Charlie's death—not *if* he would die, but *how*. He and his wife had spent such a beautiful, special time together! I hoped the memory would not be spoiled by a difficult struggle with death.

Quickly I returned to the linen closet for the third time that night and prayed that when the time came, his life might end quietly. As I knelt there, a feeling of calmness enveloped me, and I felt certain that everything would be all right.

As I was checking my other patients, the attendant with whom I was working came to find me.

"It's Charlie," he said. "I don't know if he's gone or not." I reached for a stethoscope from the nurses' station as we walked by.

Charlie was lying still on the bed. His eyes were closed; a look of serene peace graced his countenance.

"He closed his eyes as I spoke to him," his wife said. "Is he asleep?"

I placed the stethoscope on his still chest; I knew I wouldn't hear anything. I turned to them and said, "Charlie has gone home."

They wept quietly. Later I walked them to the door, letting my arms around them convey what words could not.

"Thanks for calling me," Charlie's wife whispered, squeezing my arm. "I wouldn't have missed these few hours for the world!"

Telford, "Charlie," *Ensign*, Sept. 1986, 42. © by Intellectual Reserve, Inc.

Ye shall receive the Holy Ghost,
that ye may have all things made manifest.

MOSES 8:24

"GO TO THE TEMPLE"

JAMES R. OSBORNE

I joined the Church thirty years ago. My testimony was gained through personal revelation, following study of the Book of Mormon. It has been my privilege, through most of the past thirty years, to enjoy good communication with Heavenly Father. Answers to my questions have, for the most part, been easy to achieve. A few years ago, however, for a brief period, relatively speaking, my wife and I lost this privilege.

We had gone through some tough times. I lost my job to corporate downsizing, my health failed, and although I was very active in trying to find another position, no one was really interested in hiring a fifty-plus-year-old man in poor health. Although my wife was working, her paycheck alone was not enough to sustain us. Things continued to go steadily downhill.

Our daughter, who lived in Iowa, suggested we come to live with her. We resisted this suggestion—we were very attached to our ward and neighborhood in the Salt Lake area. We prayed, together and in private, but no answers were forthcoming. The revelations I had been accustomed to receiving so easily were not there. The heavenly switchboard had become silent. Things continued to deteriorate.

Finally, about six months after my daughter suggested we move in with her, things caved in completely. In rapid succession, my wife lost her job, the car was repossessed, and our landlord told us we would need to move out. With most of our meager savings used up, no relatives in the area, no job, no transportation, and both of us in fragile health, I finally did the thing I had previously resisted. I called my home teacher and asked him to bring another member of the ward to give me a blessing.

The brethren came to the house. An interview was held and a blessing given. The blessing touched on many things, some of which those giving the blessing could not have known about, but one suggestion was particularly straightforward and specific: Go to the temple. Through lack of time, poverty, and simple neglect, we had not been to the temple for many years. Although I was a fairly active genealogist, I had for the most part been turning in my work without bothering to do it myself. In the blessing I was told I must visit the temple to receive the answers to the questions I had been asking.

By this time, out of desperation, we were already making plans to move to my daughter's place in Iowa. Nevertheless, we made arrangements to go to the temple before we left. It required a great deal of personal effort, but through dogged determination we made the short trip to the Jordan River Temple and went through the session. By the time we returned home, I had finally received the answers I had been seeking; I knew what the Lord required of me. The move was right, and blessings would flow from our obedience. But that was not all: once again I began to receive the day-to-day revelations to which I was accustomed. We made our final preparations to move and, with the help of other ward members, packed all our belongings in a rental truck to make the move to Iowa. Before we departed, we prayed that the Lord would help and protect us on our way.

Donna flew out by plane, and I left driving the truck and towing my son's car. The trip itself was another testimony to prayer. The road was far rougher than I remembered it, and the extra weight of the car carrier on the back caused the rental truck to creep at less than ten miles an hour up some of the mountain grades. By the end of the first day, I was far behind schedule. The Spirit suggested that I should stop in Laramie for gas, but relying on my own knowledge, I decided I could make it another hundred miles to Cheyenne before stopping; after all, I had almost half a tank (about twenty-five gallons) of gas. In my arrogance I had forgotten the Continental Divide. As I started up the steep road, the truck used enormous quantities of gas. Worse, there are no gas stations between Laramie and Cheyenne. I began to regret my dismissal of spiritual promptings.

Seeing a sign with a promise of gas, I turned off the highway and proceeded down a narrow one-lane road, only to find the remains of a gas station that had probably been abandoned for years. With the car carrier on the back and no place to turn around, I faced the prospect of trying to back up the truck for a mile to get to a place where I could turn around. What is worse, when I had turned off the freeway, the gas gauge had already been on empty. Now my prayers were really in earnest. It had been more than twenty years since I had driven a semi. My skills at backing with mirrors were minimal, and with the car carrier so small behind the rental truck, I could not see the trailer until it was already seriously out of line. For nearly forty minutes I backed down the road until I finally came to a wide spot where I could turn around. I knew the truck should have run out of gas long before then. Somehow, though, it didn't. Finally I got back to the freeway and started for Cheyenne again.

I used every method I knew to conserve gas, coasting when possible and being very careful with the accelerator—and always praying for help. The Lord did not totally overrule my foolishness, but he did bless me. I was only twelve miles from Cheyenne when the engine finally sputtered and died. I was unable to flag down a passing car, so I spent the night in the truck. But I was comforted that I was not stuck on that little-used side road, and the next morning I was able to flag down a ride and get gas for the truck.

We eventually got to my daughter's home, where the blessings continued. My daughter, at that time, was inactive in the Church. But as we became active in the little branch there, so did she—and she found anew the joy of the gospel of Jesus Christ. She firmly believes the reason we went to Iowa was to reactivate her, which may indeed be the case.

But there was another reason why the Lord directed us to move to that area. My father lived in Michigan. When he had a stroke a year later, we were in a position to quickly pack up and move to his place to help him. A trip from Utah to Michigan would have been out of the question, but moving from Iowa to Michigan was much easier.

As we have continued to pray and receive answers from the Lord, we have seen his blessings in many ways. We have been able to rebuild our lives while living in yet another wonderful branch. We have cried out to him about big things and small things, and he has always listened. I am grateful that in the temple and in my home, I am learning to listen as well.

The Spirit enlighteneth every man through the world, that hearkeneth to the voice of the Spirit.

D&C 84:46

"THE LORD HAS CARRIED ME"

OLIVIA HART

For most of my adult life I have enjoyed teaching Primary children. I feel I have done well at it. Teaching Primary falls well inside my comfort zone.

But that comfort was shaken when my bishop invited me into his office and asked me to do something I had never done before—teach adults. To make things worse, he called me to the most challenging adult class I can think of, which is Gospel Doctrine.

I have a testimony of the gospel. I know that the Lord inspires ward leaders when they prayerfully ask where members of their ward should serve. But could I feel that was true of me, now?

I answered with a yes, but I was nervous and worried. What could I possibly teach those in my ward who were so knowledgeable? Would those people even be open to what I tried to teach? Wasn't I too young and inexperienced to have such a calling? I feared criticism and judgment.

I returned home from my meeting with the bishop with a

resolve to obtain a witness from the Lord that this new calling was indeed his will. When I prayed, a warm feeling filled my soul, and I knew that it was right. I resolved I would do my best, but still I felt almost consumed with fear.

Before my first lesson, I prayed repeatedly and deeply for help. I studied the lesson carefully to make sure I understood the material. I tried to be open to what Heavenly Father would have me teach. I specifically asked that the Spirit of the Lord would be with me and with the members of the class so we would understand the truth and receive a witness of it. I asked for help so my insecurities did not overshadow my conviction or my ability to deliver a strong spiritual message. I asked for divine help so I would be able to deliver the lesson with sincerity and testimony.

I was surprised at what happened when I actually went to teach. I felt quite nervous before the lesson. I also felt nervous after the lesson. But during the lesson I was calm. I felt the Spirit. I felt that through the grace of the Lord I was able to teach well. I did the best I could, and he made up for the things I could not do on my own.

So it has been with each lesson I've taught. I've prepared diligently and prayerfully. I've been nervous and worried. And the Lord has carried me through the lesson, every single time.

Along the way I've learned another important lesson. Through inspiration I have learned that I should be more Christlike and loving toward those in the class rather than worrying about what they think of me. When I focus on their needs rather than my own anxieties or insecurities, I am able to receive much greater help from the Spirit. And I've discovered that when I focus on loving them instead of on my own fears, I am able to love them better, and I forget my fears for a while.

My knowledge and testimony of the scriptures have grown through this terrifying and wonderful experience. But, more important, I have gained a more complete understanding and witness of the grace of God and his love for me. I know that he can and will bless me in every capacity in my life, large and small, if I am willing and if I sincerely try to do his will.

He that hath mercy on the poor, happy is he.

PROVERBS 14:21

THE GREEN STAMP CHRISTMAS

DEBI MCMASTER

Lick 'em, stick 'em, and redeem 'em—mostly green stamps but some gold stamps. Stamps were the story of our lives. Saving those little green stamps somehow accumulated and translated into money. We loved collecting them from the grocery store and putting them in the cupboard above the fridge for a future "green stamp" day. When our mother would say we had enough, we would take the little empty books and fill the appropriate boxes with the coinciding size stamp. What a treat to have one big gold stamp fill the page versus tons of little green ones. We loved licking those stamps, even though the foul-tasting glue left a residue clinging to our tongues. After all the stamps were in their books, we would pore through the redemption catalog, dreaming of our soon-to-be acquired treasures.

Christmas was usually tight, but I remember one year when Mother had collected a whole bagful of stamp books, and we were excited to go into town and redeem them for cherished gifts. We stopped by the fabric store first, and in the hubbub of chasing after six wild children, my mother inadvertently left her bag of stamp books on a bolt of fabric. We were well on our way to the green stamp store before my mother discovered her loss and mentally retraced her steps. We returned to the fabric store and spread out to make a search. My mother knew exactly where she had left her bag, but it was nowhere to be found. She asked the clerk if she had noticed anyone picking up her coveted paper bag. She had not.

When we got back to the car, my mother burst into tears. She had saved for so long, and now all her plans faded as in a puff of smoke. We felt bad too, for all our licking was in vain. Our hearts were sick for ourselves as well as for our mom. We offered a prayer that we would be able to find our green stamps so we could have a merry Christmas. My mom felt an impression to go to the green stamp store. Leaving us in the car, my mother entered the store and immediately saw a disheveled woman carrying a familiar-looking bag. "Where did you get the bag?" Mom asked.

The woman answered with tears in her eyes. "It was a gift from heaven," she said. She explained that she was homeless and could not afford to eat, let alone buy gifts for her two children. She said she had stopped in the fabric store to get warm and there before her was the bag full of green stamps. She had prayed for help and her prayers had been answered.

When mother returned to the car, her moist eyes betrayed her. "Did you find our green stamps?" we asked.

"Yes," she replied. "We have been given a wonderful gift this year. We will do as the Savior would want us to do."

We were shocked and a little disheartened when she retold

the story of the woman with *our* green stamps! But as time passed we knew our mother was right—it truly *is* better to give than to receive. I will always have a tender heart when I see a stamp of any kind that reminds me of the year we helped Heavenly Father answer a poor woman's prayer.

Faith, hope, charity and love, with an eye single to the glory of God, qualify him for the work.

D&C 4:5

BUT HE THAT LOSETH HIS LIFE

NAME WITHHELD

One year into my mission I was assigned, as a district leader, to be the companion of an elder who had been in the mission field four or five months longer than I had. We had both served as senior companions, and he seemed somewhat offended that I was to be not only his companion but also the district leader, which effectively made me his senior companion. It was an awkward situation, and I'm sure it was quite as uncomfortable for him as it was for me. As we began to work together there were a few stumbling blocks, but most of our time together was spent working harmoniously.

One day we were teaching the gospel to a family who had been referred to us by a member of our branch. I had presented the first discussion and made an appointment to return to teach them the second. After we left their home, my companion said that he just didn't think the family was ready and that we were wasting our time teaching them. I answered that they were the best teaching situation we had at the time and that we had better spend our time working with them.

As we proceeded through the discussions with that family, my companion took a passive role in the conversion process. Instead of taking turns teaching the lesson on each visit, he withdrew his participation somewhat, requiring me to give all the discussions and to take the lead in teaching the family. As we continued to teach them they became more and more receptive until, after several weeks, they set a date to be baptized.

The day of the baptism came. That morning, as we were getting ready to leave, I couldn't find the forms we had filled out during the baptismal interviews. I had just seen them a few days before, and I knew that we had them, but now they were missing. I asked my companion if he knew where they were, and he said they were in his briefcase. I thought that was curious, but as we prayed before leaving the apartment, it became evident to me that he was planning to take over the final details of the baptism. In other words, after contributing almost nothing to the process, or to the family, he was going to step in and take over some of the most rewarding aspects of the work.

As it dawned on me what was happening, I could see the potential for ruining the baptismal day of this family if we were to argue or fight over who was to conduct the interviews and who was to perform the baptisms. I searched my mind and found comfort in the thought that the most important thing was the welfare of the family—that this day should really become a day that they would remember forever. It should be a time for being touched again by the witness of the Spirit, and I knew that the Spirit could not be present when two missionaries were being influenced by the spirit of contention. I did not want to detract from the converts' experience in any way, so I resolved, absolutely, to exert my faith in their behalf so that it would be their special day.

I remember riding along the beach in the open streetcar to the family's home and praying that they would feel the Holy Ghost touch them and testify to them, again, that this was truly the restored gospel. As I did so I felt a sweet confirmation of the Spirit that it would be a wonderful day for them and, in addition, I felt a feeling of personal contentment that I perceived was designed particularly for me. It removed from my soul any bitterness or disappointment at the course my companion had chosen. I did not feel what I had expected to feel. I was at peace. In fact, the influence of the Spirit was so sweet for me that I remember almost arguing with the Lord that what I had been asking was a witness for them, not for me. But he had recognized that two teaching opportunities existed simultaneously—a wonderful family and a young elder. He responded to both.

As we arrived in the family's home I continued that prayer, and when my companion pulled out the paperwork and began the interviews it slowly became evident to them that he would be the one to perform the baptisms that day. I was very supportive of the procedure, and as they looked my way I confirmed that my companion would be doing the baptisms and smiled in the most positive way I knew how. The baptismal interviews proceeded successfully, as did the baptisms. The day turned out to be all that

I had prayed for and was, in fact, one they can look back on as a spiritual milestone.

Now, twenty-seven years later, it is a source of real joy to know that the gospel has become precious to them. Their lives in the intervening years have been exemplary. I thank my Heavenly Father for having had the opportunity of working with this faithful family.

As I reflect back on that day and its events I hold no animosity toward a companion who engaged in some actions that were out of character for him. Instead, I remember that day as one in which we had one of our finest baptisms and in which I felt a deeper understanding of the principle reason why I was a missionary—not to register baptisms in my name but to lead families to the Savior.

From Ayres, *Great Teaching Moments*, 99–101.

My grace is sufficient for thee.

2 CORINTHIANS 12:9

JUST ONE SMALL THING

KATHRYN GAUNT

Frogs? I must have misheard her. Did she say frogs? We were going to dissect *frogs?* Logically I knew it made perfect sense for a ninth grade AP biology class assignment, but I couldn't help swallowing hard, my stomach already turning over with dread.

My lab partner, Darcy, grinned and started copying down the lab rules that Mrs. McGwire was writing on the board. Of course Darcy would be excited, I thought. She wanted to be a marine biologist. Me? I was more comfortable dissecting sentences than animals and studying poetry instead of a frog's large intestine. The idea made me feel ill. I knew that if I had to dissect a frog, I'd probably get sick right there on the lab table. What was I going to do?

"Please, Mom," I begged. "Let me stay home sick that day. I'll never ask for another thing, I promise."

Oh, please, Heavenly Father, I prayed, *make Mrs. McGwire change her mind.*

"Please, Dad," I implored. "I'll do extra credit to make up for it. I won't let it lower my grade."

Oh, please, please, Heavenly Father, I prayed, *I can't do this. Don't make me do this.*

"Class," Mrs. McGwire called for our attention, "I have an announcement to make about tomorrow's dissection assignment."

Euphoria filled my heart. This was it! She had changed her mind and we were going to do something else; I was spared!

"We do not have enough eyedroppers to go around, so not all of you will be able to inflate the frog's lungs as part of the assignment. For those of you who do not receive eyedroppers, please make sure to watch someone else perform the procedure."

I dropped my head in my hands. *Please, Heavenly Father, don't let tomorrow come.*

That night my mom came into my room and sat on the edge of my bed. "You know," she said, "sometimes when we are faced with difficult assignments it helps to pray for help."

"I've been praying nonstop," I protested. "But nothing's worked."

"Just because God can do something doesn't mean he will. But I know he will do what he can if you ask sincerely." Mom leaned down and kissed me good night.

I lay in bed for a while, thinking things over.

"Dear Heavenly Father," I whispered. "I'm sorry that I've been asking for the impossible these last few days. I know that I'm going to have to go to class tomorrow and I'm going to have to do something that is going to be very hard for me. Is there anything you can do to help me? I don't care what it is, but I'm going to need help to get through tomorrow." I paused, but I couldn't think of anything else to say. I closed my prayer and eventually fell asleep.

The next day, I stood outside the biology lab with the rest of my class. The day hadn't been any different from any other day, and I was nervous that the Lord wasn't going to answer my prayer. All too soon, Mrs. McGwire opened the door and we filed inside.

"Oh, gross!" Darcy wrinkled her nose. "What stinks in here?"

"It's the formaldehyde," our teacher explained. "It's used to preserve the frogs. I know it smells bad, but you'll get used to it."

"Yuck," another student said. "We'll *never* get used to that!"

I took an experimental breath. The air smelled normal to me. I took a deeper breath. Nothing unusual. I slowly realized that I couldn't smell the formaldehyde.

With that knowledge came an overwhelming feeling of confidence and strength. The Lord *had* answered my prayer. He wasn't going to let the school burn down, or strike my teacher with amnesia, or make the frogs disappear just so I could get out of an assignment. But he cared about me enough that he did what he could to help me. It was just one small thing, but it made all the difference. And it was enough that I was able to work with Darcy on dissecting our assigned frog.

I have forgotten most of what I learned that day about a frog's heart. But I have never forgotten what I learned about my own heart—and the Lord's.

Let thy soul delight in thy husband.

D&C 25:14

HE DID A LOT OF ANNOYING THINGS

SHANNON RICHARDS

Rob and I have been married for fifteen years. We were both prayerful before we got married, and we both felt a confirmation from the Spirit that we should marry one another. We have had difficulties like most couples. We hadn't been married long when we visited my parents, and I could feel my mother cringe when I'd talk to Rob. My mother is a wonderful, kind woman, and I knew she was cringing because of the annoyed tone I often used when talking to my husband. Once, in a kind way, she talked to me about being loving and kind when I speak to Rob. "But Mother," I said, "he just does things that make me mad." It was clear to me that he did indeed do a lot of annoying things, and it was also clear that if he would think and act more carefully, he wouldn't make me mad.

We'd been married five years when Rob nicely said to me that it would be good if I could use a different tone when I talked to him. I agreed, and I put signs up around our apartment that said "TONE" to remind me. They did little good.

We'd been married seven years when I really began to think

about why I was so often annoyed with Rob. As I pondered it, I realized that the real problem wasn't all the little careless things he did. Instead, I was upset because I felt hurt: from the beginning of our marriage he hadn't been loving and caring and treated me in the way I wanted him to treat me and had thought he would treat me. I resolved to forgive him.

However, Rob's hurtful behaviors continued, and I soon reverted to my previous pattern. Though we'd frequently, often heatedly, discuss the things that bothered me about him, he continued to be and act the same as always (with some minor modifications). I felt so angry with him that I almost always acted annoyed with him.

Our relationship got so bad that Rob and I would rarely touch or express love to each other, and usually the only things we talked about were things that were necessary to take care of our family and Church responsibilities. Sometimes we'd have big arguments.

I felt deep pain. I prayed many times, asking Heavenly Father if it was his will that we divorce. Every time I asked, I felt that divorce was not the answer. But it was so painfully difficult to stay married. Rob didn't pay much attention to me or our relationship, even though I told him I thought we didn't have a good marriage. He spent his time and effort on other things.

I began to pray for more guidance in how to act toward Rob. I thought my angry feelings toward him were not Christlike, regardless of how he was treating me. Heavenly Father helped me to understand line upon line, precept upon precept, how I should feel and act toward my imperfect husband.

One of the first things I learned was that I needed to be thankful for Rob. There are many positive things about him: he is a good father and a good provider, and he is helpful around the house. I prayed for help in being more thankful for him. I also learned that I shouldn't give up on our marriage as I had been doing.

Then, as I prayed and prayed, striving for help, I was able to imagine how Christ might feel in my situation. With his pure love, he would be more concerned about his mate's eternal progress than the fact that he wasn't being treated right. Christ would (and does) desire to help Rob in a loving, persuasive, long-suffering way. I began praying for help to love Rob in a Christlike way.

As I continued to pray and think about my feelings, trying to understand better why I acted and reacted the way I did, Heavenly Father helped me remember and piece together my innermost feelings. When I was growing up, my father treated my mother in ways that were not kind, loving, or respectful. He was anything but considerate toward her. I resolved all my life to marry a man who was not like my father. As I dated, I would purposely look for behaviors that would indicate whether that young man was like my father or not. I thought Rob wasn't anything like my father. After we were married, though, Rob began to exhibit some behaviors that were like my father's, and every time he did, I felt devastated, crushed, and angry—very angry.

Heavenly Father also helped me realize that from a young age I longed to be purely loved by a man because my father had loved me in an incomplete, selfish way.

Having realized where my devastation and hurt were coming from, I asked Heavenly Father to help me change my heart, to help me not to feel that I must have a husband who treats me perfectly in all things. I asked him to help me love Rob without worrying so much about whether he loves me enough. I continue to pray for this help, trying constantly to be better, and Heavenly Father is gradually changing me as I yield myself to him.

If there's an issue I feel Rob and I need to talk about, I pray for help to do so calmly and kindly. I pray constantly for help to forgive my husband for his flaws and mistakes. But at the same time I've prayed to recognize and improve my own flaws and mistakes. I've tried to be more Christlike toward Rob and in other aspects of my life. Before I was blaming all our problems on my husband; now I've learned that I have much to change and work on myself.

I received, and continue to receive, many blessings as I have strived to change for the better. I feel a closer relationship to my Heavenly Father; I feel more peace and joy inside; with Heavenly Father's Spirit and guidance, I'm able to handle difficult situations better.

And, much to my happiness, my husband has changed a lot as well. As I began treating him with more kindness, he began treating me with more kindness. As I began to be more loving to him, he began to be more loving to me. Our relationship is better than it has been for many years. I am so grateful for Heavenly Father's help as the two of us, both flawed and imperfect, try to build a successful marriage.

Hear instruction, and be wise, and refuse it not.

PROVERBS 8:33

"GET OFF THE TRACKS!"

WENDY R. RUDDER

The Wyoming winter had been so long and cold! It was January, and the snow was piled up to the eaves of the porch, packed solid from the weight of each successive storm.

The barn doors had long since been drifted shut. The pasture was so deeply covered with snow and drifts that a snowmobile was the only way to take the horses food and water. The horses had to stay out in the raging elements, but they didn't really seem to mind. Since the fence that contained them during the summer had been buried under frozen mounds of white for several months, they could roam at will. Their wanderings included straying along the extremely busy railroad tracks.

The ring of the telephone would alert us, again and again, that our horses were on the tracks. No matter what we tried, we couldn't keep those single-minded animals corralled.

One January evening brought, at last, some peace and quiet, and for a change, no wind. The house was warm, and the children laughed and played, making bedtime preparations a little more joyous than usual.

Then the phone rang—the horses were on the tracks again. "How am I supposed to get them back where they belong?" I thought. "My husband is at work, it's dark outside, and I don't have any transportation except for the snow machine."

I grabbed Burt's big, brown, insulated coveralls and my black overboots, wrapped a scarf around my neck, slipped a helmet on my head, and went off to chase those ornery critters back where they belonged.

I rode along, thinking I would soon find the horses. I didn't, so I decided to cross the railroad tracks, hoping to find them already back in their pasture. The tracks had been snow-packed all winter, so we had been able to skim right across. As I approached them I gave the sled full throttle so I could cross in a hurry. I will never forget what happened next.

It was too dark for me to see that the weather had warmed just enough to melt all the snow from around the tracks. I slammed to a stop, sitting crossways on the tracks, with the sled's skis firmly wedged underneath the track.

I knew I had to get that snow machine off the tracks. I pulled it, straining every muscle, all the while praying, "Help me, Heavenly Father, help me!" I pulled, looked for a train, then pulled again.

A thought came to my mind: "If a train comes around that corner you'll never hear it until it's too late. Get that helmet off your head!" I tore the helmet from my head and reached for the snowmobile again. Suddenly, the light of a freight train appeared around the bend. Then, very distinctly, I heard, "You have three children at home. *Get off the tracks!*" I immediately began to run, fearing the train would throw the sled sideways at me. The next few moments seemed like an eternity. I turned around just as the train came hurtling past. I watched it plow into the sled and throw it, like a child's toy, 150 yards down the track.

I was stunned, and for a moment I couldn't move or react. I felt sick inside, and helpless. Then came violent trembling and tears. I began walking numbly toward home, not feeling the chill winter night on my cheeks or the ice-packed road beneath my heavy boots. When I reported to the line foreman what had happened, he and his wife stared at me in disbelief. They couldn't believe I had walked away, completely unharmed, from such an accident.

The next morning, our family went to find the snow machine. Pieces were strewn everywhere. Only a twisted part of the body of the sled remained intact. Our children were very sober when they learned what had happened—and what could have happened. Our four-year-old, Travis, said in his bedtime prayer, "Thanks for keeping Mommy safe."

I know our Heavenly Father answers prayers. I also know that our prayers are not always answered in the way we expect. But in my case, I was given what I really needed. My prayer for help did not allow me to save the snow machine, but it did save my life.

Rudder, "'Get Off the Tracks!'" *Ensign*, Jan. 1988, 50. © by Intellectual Reserve, Inc.

Charity is the pure love of Christ.

MORONI 7:47

HE ANSWERED WITH ANGELS

JULIE CARON

I gave birth to my daughter, Averi, when we were living in a small town called Cottonwood, Arizona. My mother was able to be with me for the first week to help take care of our new child, but then she had to return home to Utah to care for my siblings who were still at home.

After Averi was born, I was hit with severe postpartum depression. My emotional pain was as intense as the physical pain of my difficult labor, and it worsened when my mother left. I had nothing left in me to take care of my precious daughter, let alone myself or our home. I was nearly paralyzed by my state of hopelessness and even afraid to breathe. I repeatedly cried out to my Heavenly Father, pleading for help. I was absolutely desperate. I felt that if I didn't get help immediately, I would fall into a bottomless black hole and never return.

My mom wasn't available—she lived hundreds of miles away. But I felt I should call her and tell her how I was feeling. As I talked, she realized how serious my condition was and how urgently I needed help. That was the beginning of the answer to my prayers. The Spirit prompted my mother to call the Relief Society president in my ward, Sister Winieki, and tell her my situation. My mother told her that I needed help without delay and that I shouldn't be alone. She told Sister Winieki that she would fly back down to help if needed, even though the cost of the plane ticket would be exorbitant because she wouldn't be able to buy it in advance. Sister Winieki reassured her that would not be necessary. The sisters in the ward needed this opportunity to serve me, she said.

That's when the second part of the answer to my prayers began to come. Sister Winieki called several sisters in our ward and asked them if they would each take a turn spending a four-hour shift at my home, one in the morning and one in the afternoon, until my husband, Jeff, was able to return home from work to be with me. Many sisters, young and old, were more than willing to give up time out of their busy lives, including wonderful Sister Winieki. Some of them were women I'd never even met! It was miraculous how the burden on my shoulders was lightened when they came over. I actually experienced many moments of joy in the midst of my dark depression. The sisters brought over meals, cleaned my home, took care of Averi, played board games and watched videos with me, and even brought over baby gifts. More important, they conversed with me and lent a listening ear. In the beginning I was worried that they might judge me for being too depressed to take care of my baby, but instead they loved me.

I learned a vital lesson at that time in my life. I realized just how important service is, and I continue to be humbled by the

Christlike love these sisters had for me. They were my angels, buoying me up when I felt my days were impossible to get through. In addition, a number of these sisters became my close friends, and even though I've moved back to Utah, I still keep in contact with some of them. I don't think these beloved sisters know quite what they did for me. Sometimes an act of service, no matter how small, offered at the right moment, can literally change a person's life.

There's another vital lesson I have learned from this experience. Though I was only one solitary person in a little town that is hardly more than a speck on this planet, and though I felt small and insignificant and unimportant, yet Heavenly Father heard my cry, sent a prompting of the Spirit to my mother, and then sent angels to bless me. I will never forget the kindness of these dear sisters, nor will I forget the goodness and love shown to me by my Father in those dark days of my need.

Pray . . . with all the energy of heart, that ye may be filled with this love.

MORONI 7:48

"DID I REALLY LOVE THEM?"

JOAN WALKER

Earlier in my life, I felt that one of my most discouraging traits was that I did not have a good attitude about service. When my Relief Society president called and asked me to prepare a meal or provide some other service for members of our ward, I would always do it—but not with a happy spirit. It bothered me a great deal that I didn't have a good feeling about serving others, so I began to pray for a change in attitude. Every time I was called to serve someone, my first step would be to get on my knees and ask for help in my attitude and feelings. It seemed to help, but I desired a lasting change. I wanted to come to a state where I wouldn't have to pray each time for the right attitude; I wished to be a loving person all the time.

One day as I was praying for the Lord's blessing in my service, the understanding came to me that the real issue wasn't how I felt about the service I was providing. More important was how I felt about those I was serving. Did I really love them? If I had a Christlike love for them, then serving them would not be hard.

I began to pray not only that I would be loving in each specific act of service, but also that I would also actually have the gift of charity.

I started really looking at those people I was asked to help. I asked the Lord to help me see them and feel about them as our Savior does. I asked that my heart might be changed in love, so that I could truly love them as Christ loves them. When I approached my assignments looking at the person rather than at the task, suddenly the task became insignificant, and the welfare of those I was serving became all important.

Over time my attitude changed, and I found that I no longer dreaded that call to help. In fact, I began to look forward to such opportunities. I began to find joy in serving others, and I actually started to look for ways to serve. I started to notice people around me as I shopped, waited in lines, pumped gas, and did other mundane tasks. I noticed their countenances, their words, and their actions, and I tried to find little ways to bless them, even if it was nothing more than a smile or a kind word.

Serving became more than salads and casseroles. With the Lord's blessing, I could actually feel love for people I didn't know. It became part of my heart's desire to try to bless as many people as I could. As I did, I received a wonderful and unexpected benefit. As I learned to serve others more purely, I began to feel the Savior's love for me more purely. What a great God he is! Not only does he give us what we ask in righteousness, but he also gives us much more than we could have imagined.

Beloved, let us love one another: for love is of God; and every one that loveth is born of God, and knoweth God.

1 JOHN 4:7

I BEGAN TO HAVE CRITICAL THOUGHTS

DEANNA ROSE MILLER

When my family moved into our first house in Boise, Idaho, we were so excited to finally have a home of our own. We quickly got to know our next-door neighbors, the Sorenson family. They had four children about the same ages as our four. They were a nice family and good neighbors.

It didn't take long for our children to find out how fun it was to run back and forth between houses. They would find each other in the backyard or look for each other at back doors.

It also didn't take long for me to become good friends with the mom of the family, Kristy. We were at the same stage in our lives, we were like each other in a lot of ways, and we enjoyed talking to each other. We ended up having many contacts daily, checking on our children, borrowing a stick of butter, or asking each other for advice about this or that.

After we had been there for several months, I began feeling increasingly critical of Kristy. If her children broke a toy at my house, if her children came into my house without knocking or asking, if her children came over and she didn't even know it, or if she would forget to say thank you when I had her children over, I would have a little negative thought or feeling about her.

I didn't like having such thoughts and feelings about her. Thinking rationally, I didn't think she was deserving of my criticism. She was a good person with a good family. Even if she did have weaknesses, it was not my place to judge. I knew she was trying hard to be a good mom just as I was. But still the feelings were there, and they seemed to be increasing.

So I prayed to my Father in Heaven about it. I sensed that if I could feel about Kristy the way Heavenly Father felt about her, then I wouldn't be critical of her. So I asked Heavenly Father for the gift of charity. I knew I already loved Kristy, but I wanted to love her more purely. I desired to love her as Jesus loves her. In addition to my prayers, I decided I needed to try more effectively to do my part. Whenever I would have a negative thought or feeling about Kristy, I would try to quickly get rid of it, replacing it with something else.

Perhaps I should not have been surprised at how soon I noticed a change in me. My negative thoughts and feelings were quickly replaced by a desire to serve Kristy and her family. My inner criticisms disappeared. I started to be more mindful of what her needs were, and thought about what I could do to help her.

The Sorenson family and my family have continued to enjoy each other as neighbors for many years now, and Kristy and I are still close friends. I am thankful to my Father in Heaven, who always helps me in my weaknesses, and for the answer he gave me when I prayed for greater charity for my friend.

Whosoever shall call on the name of the Lord shall be delivered.

JOEL 2:32

"BLESS US TO TRAVEL HOME IN SAFETY"

LISA MANGUM

I pulled down the gate to the bookstore where I worked and pocketed the keys. It had been a slow night at the mall, and I was closing my store alone. I slipped on my winter gloves and shouldered my backpack heavy with college textbooks and homework. Exhausted from a long day of school and a full day of work, I headed for the double doors leading to the parking lot and braced myself for the blast of cold air that waited for me. I wasn't prepared for the sight of deep snow shrouding my car in the nearly empty wasteland.

"Oh no," I whispered, "not tonight."

It must have snowed during my entire eight-hour shift. And no one had come to plow the parking lot. Thigh-high drifts of snow hunched in small mountains against the brisk, rising wind. In the distance I could see that the main intersection on State Street was crowded with cars futilely attempting to obey the flashing yellow traffic lights. Red brake lights were interspersed among white headlights as cars on the road spun in slow circles on the icy roads.

I could always unlock the store and call someone to help me, but who? Mom and Dad were in France on a business trip, and my brother was on his mission in New Zealand. I had a sinking feeling that I was on my own.

And buried under all that snow was my only way home: a ten-year-old, hand-me-down Camaro Berlinetta with balding tires and an engine overdue for an oil change. My backpack suddenly felt ten pounds heavier and the temperature ten degrees colder.

Oh, please, Father in Heaven, I prayed, *all those times I asked to travel home in safety . . . this time I really mean it.*

Sighing, I set to work digging out my car. And that was when the first miracle happened.

A dark blue truck zoomed around the corner from the mall and pulled up next to me. The engine coughed in the cold as the driver leaned out the window. "Need some help?" Out tumbled a couple of teenagers who in no time flat had cleared my car of snow and dug a pathway for my tires. They were gone as quickly as they had come, leaving me safe inside my car, waiting for the heater and the defroster to rumble into life. *Thank you, Father,* I offered up in silent prayer. *Thank you for reckless teenagers who like to spin doughnuts in empty mall parking lots. Thank you for sending them my way.*

Buoyed up in spirit, I eased my car onto the icy roads and headed for home. All the radio traffic reports contained endless accounts of accidents on all the major roads. I decided that rather than attempting the slick, steep hill leading to my neighborhood,

I would take the more gradual incline through the hospital parking lot near my home.

Bad idea. Very bad idea.

I was so close, too; that's what hurt the worst. I had maneuvered my car all the way to the last curve in the parking lot—I could even see the road leading to my house!—when it happened. I accelerated, the wheels spun, but the car didn't move. After forty-five minutes, I finally admitted to myself that I was stuck in a deserted parking lot (again! when would I learn?) and no one was coming to help me. I was alone and in serious trouble.

Leaning my head against the steering wheel, I started to cry. *Please, Father, please, I'm so close. I can't do this by myself.*

And that was when the second miracle happened.

A rap on my window startled me, and I peered through my foggy window at a man holding up a coil of rope. I rolled down my window.

"Need some help?" he asked.

I nodded. "This hasn't been one of my better days."

He looked at me more closely. "Hey, aren't you the bookstore lady?"

"What?"

"The bookstore. Down at the mall. My family shops there all the time. You helped me pick out a present for my wife last month."

"Oh. Yeah," I said, smiling through my tears. "I'm the bookstore lady." I recognized the man, though I couldn't remember his name.

He grinned and opened my door. We walked around my car, trying to figure out the best way to help me out of the snow. Together we hooked up my bulky, gray car to his large, red SUV and he towed me up the hill and out onto the highway. A blessedly clear, clean, *plowed* highway.

I've never exchanged a more heartfelt thank-you wave with anyone as I watched him drive away into the snow. *Thank you, Father. I don't know what he was doing in the back part of the hospital parking lot alone, but I don't care. And thank you for sending someone I knew—sort of.*

I turned onto my street and inched toward my home. True night had fallen long ago, and all I wanted to do was go inside and *stop driving*. It had taken me nearly two hours to traverse a route that normally took me fifteen minutes. I pulled up to my house and stopped in the middle of the street. Literally. For some reason, I thought that at the end of my ordeal, my dad would have plowed the driveway for me and my mom would be waiting up with a mug of hot chocolate. But no, my entire family was on the other side of the planet, and the house was dark and empty.

For one brief moment I contemplated giving up and just leaving my car parked where it was. But I had prayed for help, and the Lord always keeps his promises.

So maybe I shouldn't have been surprised when the third miracle happened.

My next-door neighbor opened his garage, looked at me parked in the middle of the street, then at my driveway buried knee-deep in freshly fallen powder. And he smiled. His shiny red snowblower gleamed in the soft, snowy light.

I didn't do my homework that night. I didn't do anything but curl up in my warm bed with my dog happily asleep by my legs and spend a very long time in grateful prayer to Heavenly Father for answering my sincere prayers to travel home in safety.

Hear all that the Lord our God
shall say: . . . and we will hear it, and do it.

DEUTERONOMY 5:27

"LEAVE IT ALONE"

MARILYNNE TODD LINFORD

A friend told me of a day she received two phone calls—one from the high school counselor and one from the seminary teacher. Both calls told her the same thing—that her son had been sluffing school. She felt betrayed. She had trusted this child.

He had stopped home briefly after school that day and then left. At 10:30 P.M. she had no idea where he was. He was not supposed to go out on school nights. Her anger began to increase. By 10:45 she had a plan. She would be waiting for him in the living room when he came home. By 11:00 she was nearly distraught. She had mentally created a list of unexplained actions that she wanted answers for. Being grounded for the rest of his life seemed a fitting punishment. At 11:15 she began to think he was dead someplace. At 11:30 she decided to pray to see if her planned assault on him when (or if) he came home was right. As soon as she knelt, even as she was saying the first words, the Spirit hinted to her, *Leave it alone*. She answered back, *How can I leave it alone?*

He's been sluffing school. I have no idea where he's been for hours. The thought came again, *Go to bed and leave it alone.*

She turned to go to her room, but then she heard his car. Wanting to be obedient to the prompting, she dove into bed with her clothes on. She waited. Soon there was a knock at the bedroom door. "Mom, I'm sorry I'm so late. I know you've been worried. May I come in and talk to you?" She could hear the conciliatory sound in his voice, and she invited him in. She listened. He opened up. He explained where he had been and what changes he knew were necessary in his life.

How grateful she was for the prompting and for her obedience!

Linford, *Give Mom a Standing Ovation*, 86–87.

Blessed are all they that put their trust in him.

PSALM 2:12

"WE DIDN'T HAVE THE FINANCIAL MEANS"

BECKY PREECE

When I was a junior at BYU, I decided I wanted to go on a mission. My parents were supportive in their attitude, but they didn't know how they could support me financially. They had six children and no extra money. I went home for the summer and worked and saved, trying to earn as much as I could toward my mission. I would turn twenty-one in October, and I didn't want to wait. I began to pray, as did my parents, that somehow we would have the money we needed so I could serve.

I sent my papers in and received my call in September. I was to go to the Spain Barcelona Mission; my mission would begin on November 4, 1976. I was excited. I had studied Spanish in school and had always wanted to go to Spain.

But we still didn't have the financial means to support me. My savings from my summer job would pay for all of my clothing and supplies, the two months I would spend in the Missionary Training Center, and my airfare to Spain. But the mission would cost $150 a month after that, and we simply didn't have the money. We continued to pray constantly for help.

When late October came, my mom drove me and some of my siblings to Provo, Utah. We went a few days early to see friends and family in the area. My dad had to stay home and work. Shortly before I was to enter the MTC, I got a call from my dad saying he had just been given a raise at work. It was out of the blue, totally unexpected—and it was enough to cover the cost of my mission. What a direct and concrete answer to prayer! With the Lord's blessings, they were able to send the money in faithfully every month.

I will go and do the things which the Lord hath commanded, for I know that the Lord giveth no commandments unto the children of men, save he shall prepare a way for them that they may accomplish the thing which he commandeth them.

1 NEPHI 3:7

HOW I "FOUND TIME" FOR GOSPEL STUDY

ARDELLE HOLDERNESS

A decade ago I became acutely aware of my need to know more about the scriptures. I felt I could help Jim, my nonmember husband, to understand the gospel better if I knew more about it myself.

I had been a member of the Church all my life, but like many others I had neither read nor studied as I should have. I would often say, "I'm going to read the scriptures and learn more." But that was easier said than done. We had eight children, and I had always held at least one Church position and been active in PTA and other interests. Reading seemed to be at the bottom of a long list of priorities, and time always ran out before I got to the bottom.

Finally I took this problem to my Heavenly Father. I prayed

earnestly and sincerely that I might organize my responsibilities so that I would find the necessary time for daily scripture study. Then I began reading occasionally; but it was not good enough. I continued to pray for guidance.

Meanwhile, we were planning to move from Waipahu to Hawaii Kai—a distance of about thirty miles. We had purchased a new home, and it was scheduled to be finished in about six weeks.

One day the telephone rang; it was Hawaii's seminary coordinator. He asked me if I would teach early morning seminary during the coming year. I was shocked! I had a teacher's certificate for English and math, but I just didn't know enough about the scriptures to teach seminary.

I told him that because we were moving, I couldn't accept the calling. "It's not in this area that we need you," he responded. "It's in the new area where you will be moving."

"But we won't be there for six weeks yet. If I did accept, you'd have to get another teacher until we arrived," I said, hoping to dissuade him.

"Oh, no," he answered quickly. "We don't like to change teachers in a seminary class. If you accept, we'd want you right from the beginning. You'd have to commute for six weeks."

All the objections came tumbling out: "But I've got a little four-year-old boy—and two children still in elementary school—my husband's a nonmember—he'd never let me—I'm not qualified—it's so far—I just couldn't!"

"Think about it for a few days," he said, "and discuss it with your husband." He assured me that he felt I was qualified to teach.

When I told Jim about it that evening, he wasn't as surprised as I had been. He said he thought I'd be a good seminary teacher. So we discussed the pros and cons. It was true that we wanted to get our three older children into schools in the new area at the beginning of the new school year. This would give them transportation. (Our two oldest girls, Janet and Helen, were preparing for college on the mainland.) But what about Lonnie and Darin, who were in the second and third grades? And little Patrick, who was only four? We came to the conclusion that my teaching seminary was impossible.

But after Jim had gone to work the next day, it suddenly hit me with great force that this was the answer to my prayer! This was the way Heavenly Father would help me find time to study the scriptures! What better way to "find the time" than to prepare a daily lesson for a group of teenagers? I knew the Lord was answering my prayer, and I knew I must respond.

Now, how could I tell Jim about it? How could I convince him that we could work it out? After all, we had discussed it and agreed it was impossible.

When I picked Jim up at work that day, he slid into the driver's seat—and before I could say anything he said, "You know, honey, I've been thinking about that seminary opening all day, and I think you should at least give it a try."

I couldn't believe my ears! Now, more than ever, I knew I must try.

Having my husband's support made it easier. He agreed to get Lonnie and Darin off to grade school. The rest was up to me. Each day at 5:00 A.M. I would leave for the new area with Robin and Kevin (who were of seminary age), a sleeping four-year-old, and Nancy (our eighth-grader who was not old enough for seminary) to watch him in the car while I taught. After class, little Patrick and I would leave the three teenagers at their new schools and begin the drive home. After school the teenagers would take a bus to the Institute of Religion, which was near the University of Hawaii where their father worked, and study or relax there until he could leave his office. They would arrive home with him about 6:30 P.M.

A schedule like this can be very tiring, but we thought we could manage for six weeks. Our house wasn't finished on schedule, however, and we continued to commute for three months!

But I count my blessings. If I had not recognized an answer to prayer, if I had allowed the numerous obstacles to prevent me from responding to that answer, or if I had not had the complete cooperation of my family, I would not have enjoyed the wonderful opportunity for study and growth that has come to me through teaching seminary. The bonus came in 1975 when my husband joined the Church.

I've taught in the seminary program for ten years now. The more I learn about the gospel, the more I realize I have much more to learn.

Holderness, "How I 'Found Time' for Gospel Study," *Ensign*, Sept. 1981, 66. © by Intellectual Reserve, Inc.

The Lord our God did visit us with assurances . . . he did speak peace to our souls.

ALMA 58:11

I ASKED THEM TO PRAY *HARD*

NECIA B. KITCHEN

All my life I've been taught that Heavenly Father hears and answers our prayers. We can pray for anything—for guidance in finding a lost toy, for help on a test, for peace of mind and spirit, or for the life of a loved-one to be spared. As I have put the principle of prayer to the test, my life has been blessed and my testimony strengthened daily because of answers that have come.

Perhaps my greatest trial of faith and prayer began when my younger brother, Jordan, age thirteen, was in a life-threatening accident involving an ATV. When medical staff couldn't offer encouragement or comfort, it was through prayer that peace came. When medical technology was not sufficient to bring life-saving changes, it was after prayer that miracles came to pass. Miracles and peace were the results of constant, daily prayer.

August 24, 2002, began as a normal day. Our entire family had taken a quick trip from Arizona to Provo, Utah—except for my brother Jordan, age thirteen, and sister Erica, age twelve, who had stayed home with friends in Phoenix. Mom and Dad, looking forward to some time alone, drove to Ogden, leaving the rest of us at a relative's home in Orem.

Around 1:00 P.M., I received word that something had happened at home in Phoenix and that I needed to locate my parents. Apparently Jordan had been in some sort of accident at a ward campout he had attended with the family he was staying with.

I immediately gathered my siblings around and explained the tiny bit I knew. We offered the first of many prayers that all would be well with Jordan and that Mom and Dad would return soon. A few minutes later, Kristi, the ward member Erica was staying with, called. The sound of her voice told me immediately that things were not good. Jordan and a friend had been riding an ATV, gone off the road, and hit a tree; Jordan was unconscious, and both had been life-flighted to a Flagstaff hospital; what should she tell Erica?

At first I wanted to wait until we knew more before telling Erica, but somehow I knew that wasn't fair. I explained to Erica what little I knew and told her to pray hard—to pray for Jordan, pray for the medical staff that would take care of him, and pray for Mom and Dad to get home soon. We offered the same prayer over and over as the afternoon continued.

I called both my grandmas and started calling aunts and uncles, telling them what I knew and asking them to pray hard. I knew that Jordan would need everyone's prayers and faith, even though I didn't know the extent of his injuries.

At some point I learned which hospital Jordan had been

taken to and that he had received a priesthood blessing. Knowing that a blessing had been given was very comforting. Because the hospital staff would not talk to anyone but a relative about Jordan's condition, I decided to call and see if they would talk to me.

Before I could dial Information, the phone rang. A woman at the hospital wanted to speak to my dad. I told her that he was not there and neither was my mom, but that I was Jordan's oldest sister. Could she please tell me about Jordan? All she would say was that he was in serious condition and we needed to find our parents.

Lack of specific information heightened our anxieties. We renewed our prayers—*please bless Jordan, bless our parents to return, and bless us with peace that all will turn out right.*

Eventually, around 3:00 P.M., the attending physician called. After learning I was over twenty-one, he decided to tell me about Jordan's condition. Although his blood pressure and pulse were in a good range, Jordan had not regained consciousness. He had not been breathing at the accident site, so an emergency tracheotomy was performed, allowing precious oxygen back into his lungs. At the hospital, chest tubes were inserted to drain fluid buildup, and he was put on a ventilator. His skull was fractured in several places, but the brain swelling was causing the greatest concern. My little brother was in critical condition, and all we could do was pray and wait.

When our parents finally arrived, I met them at the door, told them I had to talk to them, and asked them to sit down. I told them everything I knew. Dad called the hospital to talk to the doctor. Then he and Mom had to rush off to Salt Lake City to catch a flight to Phoenix, where Jordan had been transferred. Within four hours of hearing the news, Mom and Dad reached the hospital, greeted by concerned members of the ward and stake. They arrived barely in time to sign medical releases and kiss Jordan before he was taken into surgery.

When the surgery was over, Dad called to tell us we all needed to fly home immediately. I realized that the doctors must not expect Jordan to live. We continued to pray that Jordan's life would be spared, and that we would be comforted no matter the outcome.

We left for the airport at 5:30 the next morning. When we arrived at the hospital in Phoenix, we were exhausted and yet grateful to be there. Mom, Dad, and Erica met us with open arms. We were all together again.

I slipped into Jordan's room, alone for just a moment. It was overwhelming to see all the tubes and monitors and contraptions he was connected to. Because he had hit the tree full force with his head, his face was very swollen and scraped, and his right eye bulged out of its socket. Except for two broken bones in his wrist, the rest of his body was intact, with only surface abrasions.

I cried for him, for me, for all of us. And, yet, standing in the hospital room looking at my critically injured little brother, I felt the peaceful influence of the Spirit and I knew that everything would be all right. I didn't know whether that meant Jordan would live or die. But I knew that my prayers were being answered and I felt at peace.

Daily, family members, friends, and people we didn't even know offered prayers in Jordan's behalf. With each new setback in his progress, word was sent out to redouble our prayers and what specific thing to pray for. Through these prayers and the faith of those offering up their petitions, miracles have happened, most of which medicine could not explain.

Jordan lived through the first forty-eight hours after the accident, which on initial evaluation the doctors did not deem possible.

The growing pressure in Jordan's brain, which reached six times standard levels and sometimes more, was reduced to normal.

Within only four-and-a-half weeks of the accident, he was able to eat, read, write, and respond in ways the doctors hadn't anticipated for several months, if ever.

His therapists said Jordan was improving at a rate that was six months to a year ahead of schedule for the severity of his head injury.

After eight weeks in the hospital, Jordan finally went home and attended outpatient therapy. Nearly a year after the accident, Jordan continues to improve. He is able to walk, feed himself, read, and interact with people. He resumed his duties as a deacon, and when he turned fourteen he was ordained a teacher in the Aaronic Priesthood. Although for now he processes information at a slower rate, his knowledge is appropriate for his age, and his short-term memory and attention span continue to improve. His personality, however, has changed somewhat in interesting ways. He is more loving and generous with hugs; talks a mile a minute endlessly, even to strangers; and is concerned about what is most important in life. He is well aware of death and the importance of the gospel plan.

Our daily prayers of gratitude and our petitions for peace, comfort, and miracles continue to be answered in marvelous ways. We know Heavenly Father hears and answers the sincere, faithful prayers of his children.

Because thou hast seen thy weakness thou shalt be made strong.

ETHER 12:37

"HE JUST KNOWS HOW TO PUSH MY BUTTONS"

RACHEL JAMESON

Being a mother is never easy, but I had done well in many areas and was feeling all right about most things. However, the relationship between me and my oldest son, Garrett, was strained. We had trouble getting along in peace.

We loved each other and got along well at times, but I felt he was always opposing my decisions as a mother. Sometimes we would get into arguments. Our interactions would start out calm and then build to angry, and he would frequently end up in tears.

He would often say, "Why are you arguing with everything I say?"

I would respond with, "You're arguing with everything I say!"

I really felt that if he would stop challenging me so much we would get along fine. Yet sometimes by the end of an argument we wouldn't even remember what had started it. "Garrett just knows how to push my buttons," I would say to my friends.

I tried many approaches to this problem. I decided to try to help him understand that he could use prayer to learn when he should act differently or apologize to others. "If you humble yourself and prayerfully ask about it," I said, "Heavenly Father can help you understand what you need to do."

One day I got mad at him for something he did, and we got into an argument. Later he came to me and said, "Mom, I prayed about it, and I don't think you should have gotten mad at me about that."

Surprised, I replied, "Well, I'll pray about it."

It took a lot of humility and courage for me to pray and ask if the error was mine, and I was also worried that he might not have been open enough to learn from the Spirit that *he* was wrong. But when I finally prayed about it myself, I felt that he was right. I shouldn't have gotten mad at him.

I prayed for help because it seemed hard to admit that I was wrong. With the Lord's help, I was able to ask my son's forgiveness. I was very grateful that he had acted on the advice I had given, and I realized that I should heed my own advice. Why was I so quick to become angry with him? Why couldn't I calmly make my point and stay on track?

Garrett and I were both very prayerful in asking for help.

Over time and through a lot of prayer, I began to realize that I had a lot of responsibility in the problems Garrett and I were having. I was also able to understand some of the reasons why I was so quick to anger.

One thing I was able to learn was that I was reacting to some beliefs I had about a strong work ethic. I had been raised by parents who strongly believed that children should be hard workers. I had been taught the same thing in church. I placed a lot of value on a person who was a diligent worker. As a result, I had been so determined that my children would be hard workers that every time they were slow in doing their schoolwork or chores, I would become upset and tense inside.

Another problem Heavenly Father helped me identify was that I had a lot of pride—especially when it came to others' opinions about whether I was right. If someone disagreed with me, I would become very upset.

I came to know that with Garrett, I was often upset with him because he was working so slowly. Then much of our time in arguments was spent with me trying to convince him I was right.

I prayed and prayed for help with both issues. Now I knew why I was so often upset with Garrett, but my feelings were rooted so deeply I couldn't change them.

As I studied and prayed for help, I began to realize that the only way I could truly change was through the atonement of Jesus Christ. Our Savior's suffering not only paid for our sins, but it can also make up the difference between what we are now and what he wants us to be. If we humbly seek and plead to be changed, we can be changed.

I pled and pled to be changed to a more Christlike person. And I sought with all my might to apply the principles I was being taught. Heavenly Father heard my prayers, and the changes came.

I still have far to go, but when Garrett works slowly now I

don't feel like it's unbearable. I can talk calmly with him about problems, and I can let him be imperfect as he grows. When he opposes me, I can just make my point and stop—even if Garrett is still disagreeing with me. Truly, through prayer, obedience, and the Atonement, my heart has been changed.

I have also prayed for help to love Garrett in a Christlike way. He and I get along wonderfully now.

Garrett's prayers have also been answered. He is much kinder and slower to anger than he used to be. Our home is much more peaceful than before. I will forever be grateful for the Atonement, this gospel, and my knowledge of God and his blessings to us.

Thou hast inquired of me, and behold, as often as thou hast inquired thou hast received instruction of my Spirit.

D&C 6:14

"I KEPT A CONSTANT VIGIL"

MARJORIE LARSEN

I have a friend named Rachel who chose to give birth at home with a midwife. She had previously had three children at the hospital, but she was thrilled with her home-birth experience. I envied her. It seemed like a romantic notion and very comforting to give birth in my own bedroom. In addition, we were having some difficult times financially, and I knew we could save a lot of money by staying at home for the delivery. In addition, I myself had given birth in a hospital three times—including with one baby who was nearly twelve pounds. I reasoned that I would never need a Cesarean section, and I began to think seriously of following Rachel's example.

I prayed about the question, but I wasn't sure of the answer. I only knew that something about the idea nagged at me, and I couldn't put my finger on my feelings.

At this time our three-year-old came down with a terrible fever—close to 104 degrees. Medication didn't seem to help, and I kept a constant vigil through the night. I called the Ask-a-Nurse hotline twice in the wee hours of the morning to get advice. I was told that a virus was going around, and that since my son had no other symptoms, he would be fine as long as he was hydrated. I was somewhat reassured but still deeply concerned for my toddler's safety. I urgently cried out in prayer for guidance, and the clear answer was that he would be fine. But words came to my mind about something altogether different: "Go to the hospital to have your baby." I had prayed "Should I go to the hospital?"—meaning with my sick child—but had received an answer to something else.

I was completely stunned. The message was so strong and clear that I could not doubt it was from the Lord. I knew then that I had to go to the hospital to have my baby. (Of course, home births can be appropriate in some circumstances; the Lord was simply giving me instructions for my own needs.)

When labor began and I did go to the hospital, we learned that my baby was uniquely positioned and couldn't be moved. He was ten pounds. The doctors quickly determined that a c-section was indeed necessary. If I had been seeking to give birth at home, the emergency could have quickly become dangerous for me, my baby, or both. But because I was already in the hospital, I was at peace, things went smoothly, and all was well. I'm grateful for a God who knows the end from the beginning and who graciously gives us guidance when we seek it.

Did I not speak peace to your mind concerning the matter?

D&C 6:23

"IF I COULD HAVE JUST ONE HUG"

ANITA R. CANFIELD

The Lord *remembers* the prayers of the righteous.

My friend Chris was a busy and involved Church member—the wife of a stake missionary and mother of six. Life for them was not perfect; there were some financial stresses and the growing pains of a large family. But generally they seemed happy and full of hope and promise of celestial goals.

Then one day Chris's life began to change before her eyes, without her ability to stop it. Her husband decided he loved someone else more—in fact, a woman to whom he had introduced the gospel. There were some serious moral transgressions, and a bitter divorce seemed imminent.

Chris held on, struggling for daily strength, fighting for home, husband, and family. Eventually it became obvious the marriage was over and there would be no reconciliation.

Chris suffered. She wept and drank again and again from the bitter cup. She sought peace and counsel from others, even priesthood blessings. The weeks moved closer to court dates. Her broken heart could not be comforted. She went to the temple, and she prayed often, long, and hard.

As the finality became settled in her mind, she sought inner assurance as well. Her mother had passed away when she was a young woman. How she longed for her mother and the consoling hugs and comfort that only a mother can bring.

Alone in the temple one evening her thoughts turned again to her mother. She longed for that hug and silently prayed, "Oh Heavenly Father, if I could just have one hug, one hug from my mother. It's foolish perhaps, but in a way I guess I need to know that somebody still loves me for me."

She felt as if her self-esteem had been temporarily deposited in the divorce courtroom. Just one hug, a little inner assurance of her own worth was all she needed.

The session came to an end, and she moved into the celestial room and found an empty corner. There she retreated into her thoughts and worked with her pain as the tears quietly fell upon white satin.

As if from nowhere a woman tapped her on the shoulder, and Chris looked up. She saw the woman motion to her husband to go on without her, and then she turned to Chris and said, "Say, you look like you need a hug. Can I give you just one hug?"

Can you imagine what a healing moment that must have been?

Some months later Chris faced more weakness, more sorrow not of her own doing. She slipped back into the deadly abyss of self-pity and discouragement, even despair. She wondered if that moment in the temple had even been real. Was she just in the right place at the right time, or was this the loving touch of the Lord? Isn't it interesting how intense sorrow and pain can distort the memory of great moments of truth?

Her Sunday School class was studying the Doctrine and Covenants. One evening she picked up the book, hoping to read something that would bring more of a witness of the Lord's love for her. She offered up a prayer of hope that the words would lend her strength. She read:

> Verily, verily, I say unto thee, blessed art thou for what thou hast done; for thou hast inquired of me, and behold, as often as thou hast inquired thou hast received instruction of my Spirit. If it had not been so, thou wouldst not have come to the place where thou art at this time.
>
> Behold, thou knowest that thou hast inquired of me and I did enlighten thy mind; and now I tell thee these things that thou mayest know that thou hast been enlightened by the Spirit of truth;
>
> Yea, I tell thee, that thou mayest know that there is none else save God that knowest thy thoughts and the intents of thy heart. . . .
>
> Verily, verily, I say unto you, if you desire a further witness, cast your mind upon the night that you cried unto me in your heart, that you might know concerning the truth of these things.

> Did I not speak peace to your mind concerning the matter? What greater witness can you have than from God? (D&C 6:14–16, 22–23).

What the Lord reminded her to do was remember, because he had not forgotten her. Her prayers were being heard and answered.

Canfield, *Remember and Perish Not*, 69–71.

Remember the worth of souls is great in the sight of God.

D&C 18:10

"IT'S A WONDERFUL LIFE"

NADA MIDKIFF

In the classic film *It's a Wonderful Life*, George Bailey discovers through angelic help the worth of a soul—his own. The trials he so fervently wishes to be gone from his life in actuality prove to be opportunities to touch souls and heal lives. Like George, our influence is incalculable. We, too, will be asked to go through soul-shattering trials where our faith is stretched thin and we ask, "Why me?" Like George Bailey, each of us should seek to learn our true purpose in God's plan. I learned my own place in that plan one day when Heavenly Father granted me an opportunity to experience the lessons learned in *It's a Wonderful Life*. I was George Bailey for a day.

In the early 1990s my husband and I both worked for the largest savings and loan institution in Texas. It became entangled in the national savings and loan crisis, and all employees lost their jobs. Suddenly, both of us were without any income. I was the Relief Society president, and my husband was a counselor in the bishopric. We were forced to leave the state to look for work. Our children spent each year for the next five years in a different state. Money was scarce, and life became hard when savings and retirement funds were used up. There simply was nothing to live on. There were moments when we didn't have coats for the winter and just went without. Christmas presents were provided by the children from their baby-sitting money. Hearts grew softer, faith grew stronger, and testimonies became rock hard.

We were thrilled when my husband, Bill, landed a government job in the state of Colorado. At last we were stable! At last the trial was past! We felt that the Lord had answered our constant prayers for stability. But six months later the state went through a financial downturn, and we knew that Bill's new job was at risk.

During that time Bill received an offer to be a commercial property manager in Montana. We prayed for guidance. Should we take this new job in Montana or stay with the job in Colorado, knowing that it could be phased out in budget cuts? As we prayed, we felt a strong feeling that we should once again move. By this time, the kids were so used to moving that we had a code phrase for packing the house. We just grinned and shouted, "Man the battle stations!" Instantly, everyone would begin packing his or her room for the move. But, oh, how we prayed that this would be the last time we would shout that phrase.

In Montana, we felt that we were in our permanent home at last. I accepted a call to serve in the nursery, and Bill was called to be the Cubmaster. At that time, I thought I knew how vital each member was to the Lord's plan. But he was about to teach me how little I truly understood. It began six months later with Bill losing his job once again.

There is a fear that grips your soul when you have no income. It is a fear that only those who have tread that path can adequately describe. That fear intensified each day as I reached for the mail and saw the mounting pile of bills to be paid. There was no savings to draw upon, for we had used it up during the previous unemployment period! My hands began to shake, and it became difficult to sleep. How would we eat? How would we live? Why had this happened again? The biggest question that loomed unanswered in my heart and soul was, "Why did we feel *inspired* to come here for such a short period of time?" I prayed fervently for help to understand.

In some ways I felt as George Bailey did when he stood on a bridge and stared in despair at the darkening swirl of water far below. My life felt out of control; I felt we were adrift on the raging river of life with no help. George Bailey had an angel sent to help him; my angel took many forms. It started with a deep impression to seek a priesthood blessing. Within hours, hands were laid upon my head from a dear, concerned bishop. (Bill had returned to Colorado to seek work.) Through the bishop, the Lord promised me many wonderful blessings, but one stood out: without the bishop knowing of my concern, he told me that I would come to know why we felt inspired to move there, even though it was for a short time.

Sunday morning I arrived at church with a secret ache in my heart. No one knew our circumstances or the silent questions I carried. Suddenly a counselor in the Primary grabbed my arm and said, "Sister Midkiff! I feel I need to tell you something that has been on my mind lately. I need to tell you why you moved here. You moved here for me." She mentioned that I had borne my testimony the first month I arrived. In it, I had addressed an issue that had troubled her heart. She said that she still remembered every word I said—and proceeded to tell me. I had forgotten that I had even borne my testimony! Then she cried and said, "Nada, I asked that you be called to the nursery because you set such an example for me that I wanted to be near you." She hugged me and left my side. I stood there in utter shock in the middle of the hall.

A quiet voice whispered, "This is why you felt inspired to come—the worth of a soul."

I took several steps down the hall and passed a member of the Young Women presidency. Suddenly she turned around and asked to talk with me about my three oldest girls. Her eyes became tear-filled. She felt that my teens had improved the attitude of the Young Men and Young Women. She said, "Before you came, the youth were not very close and they were not as spiritual. They were not what you see today. Your girls radiate a special spirit. They encouraged the youth to attend the concerts, ball games, and other events of their peers. In how many wards do you see all the young men and women going to a show together? Your girls included everyone—boys and girls. They loved everyone. I want you to know that I feel you moved here to help the youth." I was speechless.

Once again I heard a quiet voice whisper, "This is why you felt inspired to come—the worth of a soul."

I think I made it three feet down the hall before the next person stopped me. Once again I was greeted with the same statement, "I want to tell you why your family moved here." This time the speaker was a father. He had a son who was difficult. Quietly, the father implored me to understand the impact my husband had had on his son. He pleaded with me to accept his deep thanks. He said, "Your husband became his friend. He would sit on the church lawn and counsel my son. Your husband loved him, and my son knew it. I want you to know that you moved here for my son."

Once again, I seemed to hear the Spirit teach me, "This is why you felt inspired to come—the worth of a soul."

As I progressed through the day, there was scarcely a single soul I passed that did not stop to tell me why we had moved there. After the meetings were over, the bishop asked if he could speak with me. He did not know that I was George Bailey that day. He did not know that a priesthood blessing was being fulfilled. He did not know of my prayer asking Heavenly Father for understanding. He too talked about our influence on his life, how we had helped him as a bishop, and how he had been touched by our ability to see the blessings that come through trials.

As I walked out of his office the miracle continued. The mayor of the city was in the hall, and he stopped and spoke with me; a college boy called out for me to stop and chat; and a family wanted to invite us to dinner for helping their son. I was in a state of shock; even members of the ward whose names I had not learned stopped to tell me why we moved there.

I had not realized that our family had been of assistance to anyone! Tears began to fill my eyes. Through a miracle I learned the worth of a soul. Like George Bailey, I came to see the impact that we all have on the lives of others. It does not matter what calling we have in the Church, or even if we have a calling at all—we influence people's lives far, far more than we can comprehend.

That day our Father in Heaven answered my prayers and taught me that our own trials are often nothing more than opportunities to touch souls and heal lives. In the process, my own soul was touched, and my own life was healed.

Lord, my heart is exceedingly sorrowful;
wilt thou comfort my soul in Christ.

ALMA 31:31

AN ANSWER IN THE NIGHT

ELIZA ST. JAMES

Many parents know all too well the pain of a child who chooses not to accept or live the truths of the gospel.

I had such a son. He had been taught the truth. We had tried to set proper examples for him, and we did fairly well with family home evening, family prayer, and scripture study. During his young life we had taken him to Sunday meetings and other church activities.

Nevertheless, his teenage years were filled with late-night parties and rowdy friends and unwise decisions.

We tried many ways to reach him and bring him back into activity in the Church. We always welcomed him and loved him, but it seemed that our efforts bore no fruit.

How does a parent deal with such heartache?

One night I fell to my knees and began to pour out my soul to my Heavenly Father. I knew our son was a good person. I knew he was throwing away those things that would make him happy. I longed for him to receive the love of his earthly and Heavenly

Parents and to embrace the blessings of the gospel. My pleadings were long and heartfelt, accompanied by many tears.

As I knelt there in the dark, my Father in Heaven sent into my mind some distinct words that brought with them the sweet assurance that he knew me, that he heard my prayer, and that he understood my pain. These were the words: "I understand perfectly. Did I not lose one-third?"

Not only did those words bring comfort and strength, but also from that time on I understood a little better how our Heavenly Father feels when we, like some of our loved ones here, choose to decline the invitations and blessings he so freely offers us.

He that is slow to anger is better than the mighty;
and he that ruleth his spirit than he that taketh a city.

PROVERBS 16:32

I LEARNED WHY I WAS ANGRY

VANESSA SNOW

My husband and I recently went through a difficult time financially. It was a trial that taught me a lot about things more important than money.

The trial began when our family business failed and my husband had to get a new job at a much lower salary. Before long we were suffering worse financially than we had ever suffered before. In the past we had always been careful with our money and tried to make smart financial decisions. We tried to follow the prophet's counsel and stay out of debt. Now we were in a position where we couldn't even buy food or school clothes for our large family unless we used our credit card.

Sometimes we were unable to pay even the minimum payment on our credit card bill. Our credit card company cut us off. Our water heater went out, and we honestly had no idea how we could possibly come up with $300 to replace it. Thankfully, a family member scraped together the money to help us get a water heater, knowing we'd be unable to pay it back. Then our furnace went out. We were able to get a loan through the gas company to get a new one.

It was really hard on us to be in such a difficult position. We hated the fact that we were sinking into a hole of debt. We hated not being self-sufficient. We hated worrying about how we would pay for school clothes and food. We rarely talked about how hard it was because whenever we did, it was a tense and oftentimes volatile situation.

My husband had trusted me to take care of the majority of the bills and financial arrangements. Even though we rarely talked about our financial struggles, since our situation dragged on and on, we had several heated discussions. They would usually begin with my husband asking me about our financial position on bills and debts. Then, as we talked, he and I would both tense up. He would accuse me of not managing things well, or of making decisions without involving him, and I would react in anger. Often when we were avoiding talking about our finances, I would still feel frustrated and angry with him just by thinking about his attitudes and feelings.

I would also get mad at him if he bought something I didn't feel we needed. If I bought something he disagreed with, I would become angry when he challenged me.

As time dragged on and we had several discussions, always following the same pattern, I began to wonder about my anger. Why did I get so mad? Why couldn't I talk with my husband about these things and stay calm? Would Jesus be acting like this if he were in the same situation?

I began to pray not only about our finances but also about my behavior.

I asked the Lord to help me understand my own feelings and actions. It took a lot of time, prayer, and introspection. I realized that much of my anger was motivated by control. I had never thought I was controlling, but I had recognized it in others. Recognizing negative attributes in others is so much easier than recognizing them in myself. When I got angry with my husband, he would often back off, and I would get my way.

But if I manipulated him, how could my husband be free to choose? He had a stewardship as much as I did. It wasn't right to take it over and not let him be a part of our financial decisions. I realized I was controlling in other ways too, with both my husband and our children. I asked Heavenly Father to help me not be this way. As I prayed for help, I felt that I should express my opinion and then allow my husband to make decisions without being angry at him even if I believed he was wrong. I felt I should listen to his ideas and not cut him off or tell him he was wrong.

I also learned, with Heavenly Father's help, that I had a lot of pride. When my husband disagreed with me, I would get angry simply because he thought I was wrong. I hated it when he thought I was wrong.

Knowing what I should do and doing it are two different things. I prayed for help constantly. I prayed for Heavenly Father to change my heart, and then I tried with all my soul to act as I should. Slowly, slowly, through much prayer, Heavenly Father changed my heart so I could be more like the person I was trying so hard to act like. I'm still flawed, and I notice myself feeling a desire to control sometimes or feeling upset if someone thinks I'm wrong about something. I pray a lot, and I continue to receive much help.

When my husband felt I was listening to him and not shutting him down, he was much calmer and kinder about our whole situation. He became a lot more agreeable too. As we worked together, seeking and following the inspiration the Lord sent to us, we began to prosper again. We've been able to pay off our creditors, and we're thrilled to now be debt free—all except our house.

Although this experience was hard, I feel I've been blessed with true spiritual growth. I'm grateful Heavenly Father used this trial to teach me how I needed to change.

Every man shall hear the fulness of the gospel in his own tongue, and in his own language, . . . by the administration of the Comforter, shed forth upon them for the revelation of Jesus Christ.

D&C 90:11

THE VOICE SPOKE SPANISH

LUIS V. ESPINOZA

Although I kept a journal before I joined the Church, a special experience of mine in 1968 firmly convinced me of the power of a journal as a means of preserving sacred experiences for the teaching and motivation of my family.

I had joined the Church six years earlier in Chile, then moved to Utah, where I married my wife, Cleria. In 1968 I was a student, and our son Luis was three years old.

In a way, we were a family looking for a better way of living—and somewhat confused about our goals, about how to work out problems of today's world. We had fasted and prayed, and I was thinking about our problems while shaving one morning when I found myself longing for some guidance from the Spirit. I guess my mind must have been in tune just then, because I heard a voice speaking to me in Spanish. It told me exactly what I should do about our difficulties, and it made clear to me several gospel principles that we needed to understand and apply to make these solutions work in our lives.

Along with the instruction came the clear feeling that I should share this new light with my wife. I came out of the bathroom, my face still covered with lather, and exclaimed, "I have something to tell you that can't wait!" I'm sure that part of the blessing of that morning was that I could explain to her very clearly those principles about which we had been unclear—principles involving our family and the counsel we had just received in the Church concerning family home evening. This has had a great impact on our lives and has been an inspiration up to this very time, not only in family matters but also as a reminder that our Heavenly Father is watching over us and listening to our prayers.

When we read the account in my journal now, it brings back almost the same feeling that was there when it happened. Elder Hugh B. Brown said:

"Sometimes during solitude I hear truth spoken with clarity and freshness; uncolored and untranslated it speaks from within myself in a language original but inarticulate, heard only with the soul, and I realize I brought it with me, was never taught it nor can I effectively teach it to another." (*Eternal Quest*, 435.)

That is what my experience was like for me. I felt that the voice of truth was speaking to me; I felt comfortable with it; and I felt at ease. I knew it was true, and I feel so again whenever I read over my own account of it.

The fact that this inspiration came in my native Spanish

language even though I speak English was in itself an inspiration to me. Obviously the Spirit has command of all language.

Perhaps because the answer to prayer had come so powerfully and clearly, it seemed too sacred and personal for me to commit to words, and months passed without my recording it in the journal I was keeping at the time.

Then I remembered another spiritual experience I had had years earlier, just before my baptism. I hadn't written that in my journal, either, and now I couldn't remember enough details of the story to retell it. I wanted to share that event with my son—and because I hadn't recorded it, I could not.

I decided not to let that happen with this recent answer to prayer. And, as I wrote the story into my journal, I realized that without my knowing it, a few details had slipped from my memory—after just a few months it was hard to remember several things. What if I had waited any longer! But now my family has a record of the Lord's love for us. We have read it several times together, and members of my family have referred to it for their own guidance.

My eleven-year-old son has been keeping a journal of his own for five years—a good start on having a lifetime of memories always within reach, where his own past can be a strength for the present and a guide for the future.

Espinoza, "The Voice Spoke Spanish," *Ensign*, Jan. 1977, 24. © by Intellectual Reserve, Inc.

Be thou humble; and the Lord thy God shall lead thee by the hand, and give thee answer to thy prayers.

D&C 112:10

HE EXPLAINED THE MISSIONARY PROGRAM

REBEKAH JACOBS

When our oldest son, Alan, was preparing for his mission, my husband and I had great concern about how we would pay for his expenses each month. While my husband had his own business, it was not doing very well, and we had made a business investment that had left us thousands of dollars in debt to the bank. We worried about how we would be able to support our seven children, send Alan on a mission, and still meet our other financial obligations. We spent many hours in prayer struggling with this problem, seeking guidance, and asking for help. We didn't feel that we should approach the bishop with our concerns until we had exhausted all other resources.

As we thought through our expenses, we figured we'd be able to pay the interest on our business debt each month, but no more. Meanwhile, the bank was pressuring us to make larger payments in order to lower the principal balance. We felt my husband should meet with the bank officer to discuss our financial situation. We prayed before he went, asking again for help.

During the meeting with the bank officer, my husband felt inspired to talk to him about our son's mission. He told him about Alan's desire to serve our church and preach the gospel for two years. He explained that a mission was voluntary service and that Alan wouldn't have any income during those two years. He further explained that Alan would pay his own way as much as he could and that we would also make a significant monthly contribution to his mission.

The bank officer listened attentively and asked several questions about the Church, the missionary program, and what was expected of the young men as missionaries. At the end of this discussion, he accepted the interest-only payment we had been able to come up with. But he did not agree to any such arrangement in the future.

My husband was pretty discouraged when he returned from the meeting. We again turned to the Lord in prayer. We asked him for a small miracle, if that was according to his will. We asked him to help us find a way to meet our financial obligations, particularly our need to support our son.

Within the week we received a letter from the loan officer at the bank. He told us that as long as we would make regular payments on the loan's principal (he didn't even specify a particular amount), the interest on the loan would be forgiven. That was fourteen years ago; in four more months we will be making the final payment on that loan. During those fourteen years, the loan officer has changed at the bank several times, but each one has continued with the policy stated in the letter.

I know not by what methods rare
But this I know: God answers prayer.
I know that he has given his word
Which tells me prayer is always heard
And will be answered soon or late
And so I pray, and calmly wait.
I know not if the blessings sought
Will come just in the way I thought
But leave my prayers with him alone
Whose will is wiser than my own;
Assured that he will grant my quest
Or send some answer far more blessed.

Eliza M. Hickok

Be humble, . . . asking for whatsoever things ye stand in need, both spiritual and temporal; always returning thanks unto God.

ALMA 7:23

LOCKER TROUBLE

ZACHARIAH MURDOCH

I remember making the transition from elementary school to junior high. I remember getting excited because instead of one teacher, I would have six. Instead of one long class period, I would have six shorter ones, each dedicated to the study of one specific subject. What I was most excited about, though, was getting my own locker.

The first day of school I went straight to my locker to see if the combination they had given me would work. It took me a couple of tries, but after a few times opening the locker became second nature. I wanted to leave all my books in my locker so I would feel I was using it to its full potential, but I needed my books for class—so I left everything I could do without and went happily to class.

As happens with all new and exciting things, the locker lost its luster with time. It became just a mundane part of my life. Well into the semester I hardly used it, as I knew which books I could leave at home and had plenty of room in my backpack to carry the rest around. Besides, I figured if I didn't have to go to my locker between every class period, I would have more time to devote to the social aspects of junior high.

On the last day of class before Christmas, we got out early after finals. At the end of the day some friends invited me to play basketball. I stashed my backpack into my locker and went off to play. After the game, I decided to leave my backpack at school, knowing that I would need none of its contents over Christmas break.

Before I knew it, the break was over and I stood in front of my locker. Unfortunately, I could not remember my locker combination. I tried every possible combination of what I thought were the correct numbers, but to no avail. Several minutes passed with me trying my luck, spinning the numbered dial again and again. I saw the halls empty and heard the tardy bell ring.

I wasn't sure what to do. All my books were in my locker, it was the first day of a new semester, and I was already late to class. In a last-ditch effort I tried the combination again, but the outcome was the same.

It was then I decided I needed some help from above. I realized that opening my locker wouldn't be placed very high on a list of prayers to answer, were such a list to be made, but I also remembered learning that no matter what the issue, if we pray, our Heavenly Father will listen.

I uttered a discreet prayer, asking earnestly that I be able to open my locker. When I was finished I waited, but no numbers were entering my head. I waited and listened; when nothing came I decided I would try one last time. As I did so, I found that my hands, not my head, were remembering the combination. As my hands worked, I paid close attention, relearning the combination and storing the numbers once again in my memory.

As I grabbed my books and ran to my assigned room, I stopped long enough to pronounce my thanks that an all-powerful God had cared enough to help his son open a locker and get to class.

Whosoever shall put their trust in God shall be supported in their trials, and their troubles, and their afflictions, and shall be lifted up at the last day.

ALMA 36:3

"I DIDN'T KNOW WHAT ELSE TO DO"

ANN MARIE MEADOWS

My son Joe and his wife, Susan, had serious marital difficulties almost from the beginning of their marriage. Finally, after nine years, Joe couldn't take it anymore, and he moved out of the house. He said he wouldn't return home until he saw signs of a change.

Joe and Susan visited with their bishop about their problems, and the bishop referred them to LDS Family Services. They had to wait almost a week and a half before a counselor could see them. Joe was excited to finally have the opportunity to express his feelings and get some help. Meanwhile, he was staying with a friend, sleeping on the couch.

But when the session with the counselor finally came, it was a great disappointment for Joe. He came to see me afterward. He was in tears. It broke my heart to see my grown son so sad and discouraged. He said that every time he tried to explain his feelings, Susan became defensive and argumentative. She wouldn't let him speak without loud interruptions. Joe felt homesick and discouraged. Even though he visited his children every night, he really missed them. But he was convinced that if he moved back home too soon, the problems would only continue.

Joe and Susan made an appointment to see the counselor again in two weeks, the soonest she could see them. Even though the first appointment had not gone well, Joe wanted to try again. But he didn't know how he could wait that long to begin to see improvement. Two more weeks away from his family felt like an eternity.

My heart ached as we stood and discussed the situation. I wanted so badly to help, but I didn't know what to do. I felt desperate for him. I told Joe I would pray for him. I said I didn't know what else to do, but that I did have confidence in prayer.

All the next morning and into the afternoon I thought about Joe and prayed. I pleaded with Heavenly Father that somehow the way would be opened so Joe and Susan could have an opportunity to meet with their counselor to work through their problems without waiting two more weeks.

Late in the afternoon Joe called me on the telephone. I immediately sensed the relief in his voice. He told me that the counselor had had a cancellation and that he and Susan would be able to see her the very next morning. She had another cancellation the following week, and she scheduled them for that time as well.

The second session went much better, as did the third. I

could hear the hope returning to my son's voice when he called me after each visit.

Joe and Susan still have their problems, but they have worked hard together and have made real progress. Joe has returned home, and their marriage seems to be stronger and sweeter than it has ever been. They continue to see a counselor, trying to be more honest with each other and with themselves about the causes of difficulty in their marriage—and trying to be soft of heart in the process.

I am so grateful that our Heavenly Father heard our prayers and that he answered them so quickly, showing his pure love for this son and daughter who were struggling. I know that some prayers don't appear to be answered for months or years. But I know he always loves us and helps us along the way, whether the answers come quickly or over time.

I thank my great God that he has given us a portion of his Spirit to soften our hearts.

ALMA 24:8

We Talked in Whispers

Myrna Behunin

It was about a week after we had taken ten-year-old Wayne into our home through the Church Indian Placement Program. He was a bright, handsome little boy, but, of course, he had to prove himself to the other boys. He fought with them quite often, and he could hold his own with the best of them.

One day I received a phone call from his schoolteacher. The teacher informed me that he was having trouble with Wayne at school. Wayne was disrespectful to him and to other teachers. This was a blow to me. I had never had a problem like that with my own children, and it greatly upset me. Of course my temper flared, as it so often does, and I began to rehearse all the things I was going to tell Wayne when he returned home from school. "I must nip this problem in the bud," I told myself.

To make matters worse, Wayne was late coming home from school because of a fight with a neighbor boy. They fought all the way from the bus stop. Finally they were on our front lawn. Both of them were fighting rough. I watched for a while until I was sure that the fight was indeed serious. Then I stepped to the door and called Wayne into the house.

He ignored me. He was not about to back down from the other boy. As I watched, I became even more angry. I *ordered* Wayne into the house. I was so angry that I knew I could not deal with the problem while in that state, so I sent him into his room to read.

Shaking with anger, I slipped into my own bedroom and knelt and prayed. I prayed for wisdom in handling the problem, and I also asked that through the Spirit I would know what to say. As I stood up after praying, I felt a warm, calm feeling consume me. It started at my head and gently flowed to my feet.

As I opened the door to Wayne's room and saw him sitting there on the edge of the bed with a book in his hands, a million thoughts raced through my mind. He looked so out of place sitting in that room; somehow he belonged outdoors where he could run free, as he was used to doing. In an instant my heart went out to this little fellow so all alone, a little boy uprooted from familiar surroundings and plopped down in a different world, to live by different rules. He had to prove to the other boys that he was just as good, if not better, than they.

I sat on the edge of the bed next to him and put my arm around his shoulders. The first words I spoke surprised even me, for I said, "Wayne, forgive me for being so cross with you." Then I told him of the phone call from his teacher and gave him an opportunity to explain himself. We had a wonderful talk; he confided in me, and as we spoke, we did so in whispers. This was much different from the tone I had expected to use before asking my Heavenly Father for help. It was a truly spiritual experience, and it did more for the relationship between Wayne and me than any other thing.

Thank goodness we have prayer and the gift of the Holy Spirit to guide us if we ask for it.

Behunin, "We Talked in Whispers," *Ensign*, Jan. 1976, 51.

Trust in the Lord with all thine heart;
and lean not unto thine own understanding.

PROVERBS 3:5

DO YOU WANT A DAUGHTER OR A GRADUATE?

FLORENCE MARIE JOHNSON

My daughter (I'll call her Janet) was a senior in high school, and graduation was fast approaching. She must have been experiencing some spring fever (or senior fever), because she began to have a difficult time applying herself and was lagging behind on her homework.

I am a teacher by profession and therefore was well acquainted with her teachers. I knew of her neglect and attitude. I was embarrassed because these were my associates, and my children had always done well in school. Now Janet was breaking the pattern.

We talked about it repeatedly. Her indifference to doing her homework became a real issue in our relationship. I found I was constantly checking up on her, putting restrictions on her activities, and arguing about her failure to keep up with her schoolwork. I tried to explain as clearly as I could why it was important for her to do better in school. The choices she was making would have far-reaching consequences. But she didn't seem to care.

After one especially hard evening, in which we argued at length and both said many unkind things, I went to my bedroom, got on my knees, and prayed for help. I explained to Heavenly Father what Janet was doing and what I was sure the consequences would be. She might not get into a good college; she might not get into college at all; she was establishing poor habits for school and for life; she might end up in a minimum-wage job for years. Having laid the groundwork, I asked the Lord to help Janet want to do better—and to help me know how to deal with her better.

I expected reassurance that I was on the right course and that Janet needed to repent and do better. Instead, I was taken aback when the Lord's words came to my mind: "Would you rather have a high school graduate or a daughter?"

As I pondered the meaning of these words, I gradually came to understand the message. I had been placing greater importance on homework than on the priceless relationship with my daughter. My relationship with my daughter was designed to last forever. My having a positive and loving relationship with Janet was clearly more far-reaching and important than whether or not she did her homework. And it was certainly more important than helping me look good to my peers.

After much soul-searching, I repented, backed off, and tried to be more loving toward Janet. Our relationship started to improve. In the few months we had left before she moved away from home, we began to close some of the distance that had come between us. I tried to change what I focused on in our relationship, and it truly made a difference.

Today our relationship is truly sweet. She is loving and attentive to me. She blesses my life in many ways. I am so grateful for the Lord's answer to my prayer, even though it was not what I expected or even wanted to hear. I am grateful for a loving and kind Heavenly Father who provided me with a way to preserve and enhance the love between me and my daughter.

All thy children shall be taught of the Lord;
and great shall be the peace of thy children.

ISAIAH 54:13

FINALLY I PRAYED FOR HELP

LATRISHA GORDON

I am a mother of five children. As my children started to grow older, I began to think about how I was when I was young. I remembered how challenging it was to always make the right choices. I have many regrets about my behavior when I was young, and I wanted to help my children do better. How could I help my kids understand the importance of treating others with kindness? How could I teach them to make the right choices even when it's terribly hard? How could I convince them that what their peers think of them should not influence how they think and act—and how they feel about themselves?

I worried about these things for many months, praying for an answer. One day I went to a stake Relief Society women's conference. One of the speakers was from the Relief Society general board. She spoke about the very things I had questions about, and she quoted the prophets as saying that if we had daily family prayer, daily scripture study, and weekly family home evening, our children would be faithful and strong. I knew this was the solution I was looking for. This is what my children needed. They needed a sure testimony of the gospel and of God's love—and the prophets had given us direction on how to help children come to that. I resolved to do those three things.

We started immediately. Regular family prayer and family home evening were relatively easy to instigate. In the past we had been fairly consistent in both of these things, and we simply had to do a little better.

But scripture study was much more difficult. We tried many different times of day and many different approaches. It seemed that there were always insurmountable obstacles. We were tired, or we'd forget, or my husband would work late, or there would be something pressing we needed to get done. The result was that we fairly consistently failed to take time for scriptures. We tried again and again, but any kind of consistency seemed too hard—almost impossible.

Finally I did what I should have been doing from the beginning. I prayed for help. I began to ask Heavenly Father to please help us accomplish this important goal of having daily scripture study, as his prophet had asked us to do. The blessing we sought came quietly and quickly. Things truly changed dramatically, but I can't even say how or why. All I know is that the Lord began to bless us, and it made a huge difference.

We easily established a time and place where we had scripture study every day, with only rare exceptions. It smoothly became routine. It did not seem burdensome or too time consuming.

Since then we have continued our family scripture study with great success. I have learned that Heavenly Father wants to help us in all aspects of our lives, and that he desires for us to turn to him in prayer instead of fruitlessly struggling to do things ourselves. Through asking him constantly for help, our family has received many, many blessings, for which I am deeply grateful.

If ye would hearken unto the Spirit which teacheth a man to pray ye would know that ye must pray.

2 NEPHI 32:8

"I JUST CAN'T PRAY"

R. SCOTT SIMMONS

As a seminary teacher I once invited my classes to pray morning and night for an entire week, and then at the end of the week we had a testimony meeting on prayer where my students shared their experiences. Everyone in each of my classes shared something with us except for one young woman—one young woman whom I never would have expected not to pray. And so after class I caught her and said, "Hey, what happened? What's up? Why didn't you pray?" And she replied, "Oh, Brother Simmons, I just can't. I just can't pray." I challenged her to try again. And she said, "I will." But when she came back and I asked her about it, she sadly answered that she hadn't been able to.

So we stepped into my office. And I said, "You have got to tell me what in the world could be so serious that you couldn't pray." And then it came out. She didn't tell me any specifics, because I asked her not to and because that's not my place. She had done some things that had caused her to feel unworthy, to feel that she couldn't approach her Father in Heaven in prayer. Well, immediately I had her turn to 2 Nephi 32. Verse 8 says, "And now, my beloved brethren, I perceive that ye ponder still in your hearts; and it grieveth me that I must speak concerning this thing. For if ye would hearken unto the Spirit which teacheth a man to pray ye would know ye must pray; for the evil spirit teacheth not a man to pray, but teacheth him that he must not pray."

So, if you ever feel that you can't pray, where does that feeling come from? It comes from the adversary. Your Father in Heaven would never, under any circumstances, want you not to pray to him; but the adversary would. The adversary doesn't want you to have the experiences that come with prayer. He doesn't want you to feel God's love, because he knows that when you do, the Spirit will invite you to change.

I continued talking to this young lady by reading verse 9: "But behold, I say unto you that ye must pray always, and not faint." In Old English the word *faint* essentially means to "give up." So we need to pray always and not give up.

And so I said to her, "I'll tell you what—let's you and I pray right now. I'll offer a prayer and then you offer one. How does that sound?"

"Okay," she said. And so we knelt down, and I prayed a really simple prayer: "Heavenly Father, help her to know how much she's loved." And then I said to her, "Okay, go." And she said, "My dear Heavenly Father," and then she just started to sob. And finally she said, "In the name of Jesus Christ, amen." That was her whole prayer. But when she stood up, all she could say to me over and over again was, "Brother Simmons, he still loves me. He still loves me."

Adapted from Simmons, *Draw Near unto Me* (audiotape).

Delight thyself also in the Lord;
and he shall give thee the desires of thine heart.

PSALM 37:4

WE PRAYED FOR A HOUSE

BONNIE MCINTYRE

My husband, John, and I bought our first home in Utah just after we were married. We were able to get a good interest rate with the GI Bill, which helped veterans buy a home with a low down payment and low interest. After that first little home, we moved to Idaho and bought two other homes. Each time, we used the equity in our current home to buy a slightly better home.

After we had been married for twelve years, John lost his job. He tried for almost a year to find another job in the area, but nothing ever worked out. We became very discouraged with the prospects in Idaho and finally decided to move back to Utah. We knew we would have to rent until John found a job and we could buy another house. We hated the idea of renting. We had enjoyed having our own house to decorate and remodel. It seemed in some ways that renting a house was a waste of money—we wouldn't be building equity, but all the money would be going straight to the landlord. But because of our financial circumstances, we had no choice. We looked around, found a fairly decent house to rent, and moved in. By this time we had six children.

John continued to look for work without any results. We lived on the equity from our Idaho house while he was job hunting. I felt that our house was only a temporary residence, and so I had a hard time feeling settled. I didn't want to get too involved in the schools or the ward, always thinking that we would soon be purchasing a new home and moving. I kept all of the boxes we used to move to Utah so I wouldn't have to find new ones when the time to move again came. Nearly a quarter of the basement was stacked with empty boxes. The children loved to play in them, to make tunnels and play hide-and-seek. I would repeatedly tell them to be careful not to ruin the boxes because we would need them to move again. Every day I asked Heavenly Father to please help us find a way to buy our own home again.

Five years later we were still in the same rented house. (I finally threw away the boxes.) John had found work and was diligent in his job, but he had not been able to find employment that matched his skills. My dreams of having another home of our own were fading. I didn't see how we could ever possibly buy a home again. The price of homes had gone way up. Our opportunity with the GI Bill was used up. We couldn't have come up with a down payment, and we didn't have the credit to buy a house. I didn't see how my prayers could ever be answered. My fervent requests in prayer continued, but they gradually became less frequent.

Still, the Lord works in mysterious ways.

Our landlord was continually cross because he hated coming over to do home repairs. Our children annoyed him. He tried to sell the house but had no luck. Then one day he told us that he was sick and tired of our old house. He didn't want to be responsible for it anymore. He told us that we could buy the house and take over the payments if we would just pay the closing costs. Even that was more than we had—about $500—but it seemed so important that we put it on a credit card. The house payment was about $25 a month less than what we had been paying in rent.

It has been nineteen years since we moved here, and we are still in the same house. Most of our children are now gone, having attended the same ward and the same school for most of their lives. We have remodeled our home several times and made it into a cozy little nest for ourselves. We have built up equity to put toward our retirement.

I often think of the miraculous blessing the Lord gave to us in providing an opportunity for us to own a home again. The home we have is not what I would have dreamed of having. It's old and small and doesn't have all the latest features in architecture and comfort. But we honestly don't care because the home we're in is ours, and we love it, and we're forever grateful that our Father in Heaven provided us with a nice home in a nice ward, a place where we could put down roots and grow together.

He will preserve the righteous by his power.

1 NEPHI 22:17

STOP!

MICHAEL D. PARRY

One of my favorite winter pastimes is to go snowmobiling with friends in the high mountainous country of Utah. We always start with a prayer. Snowmobiling has its dangers—and in addition to being careful, we knew we needed protection from our Heavenly Father.

One day we went out in weather that was a little marginal. Clouds rolled in and out, and we experienced several small snow scurries. When the weather is cloudy and snowy, the landscape becomes very "flat" and difficult to see. You literally can't tell if you are going uphill or downhill, and it is difficult to see any distance. We had been fighting this condition for quite a while, and we were getting impatient to get on with our ride. The country was familiar to us, but as we rode along, a cloud blew in and created this "flat" condition.

I was in the lead, and suddenly I had a strong impression that we needed to stop. Halting immediately, I put my hand up to warn those behind me to do the same. We sat on our snowmobiles for several moments, waiting for the storm to abate. When it had cleared somewhat, I got off my snowmobile and walked very carefully ahead. Trudging through the snow for about fifteen feet, I saw that I was on the edge of a very steep drop-off. If I had not heeded the impression to stop, we all could have been seriously hurt and possibly killed. As it was, we were able to turn our machines around and find a safe way out.

I am thankful for a Heavenly Father who loves us and protects us from harm. He hears our prayers and blesses us in so many wonderful ways.

Ye must press forward with a steadfastness in Christ, having a perfect brightness of hope, and a love of God and of all men. Wherefore, if ye shall press forward, feasting upon the word of Christ, and endure to the end, . . . Ye shall have eternal life.

2 NEPHI 31:20

I WAS A BISHOP BEFORE I REALLY LEARNED TO PRAY

RICHARD D. ANTHONY

My personal goal had been to read the Book of Mormon at least once a year. At each reading I became greatly impressed by the experience of Enos—his forthrightness and persistence in seeking the Lord all the day and night, without ceasing, until he received an answer; his concern first for his own soul before he could be of help to others. I was moved by the great visions of the brother of Jared. His three-hour experience with the Lord in which he was chastened for not praying regularly was both exciting and sobering.

I, too, desired closer communion with my Father, but while my prayers were dutiful and regular, I had never made the effort of an Enos to really communicate.

Upon receiving a call to be branch president, I decided the

time had come for me to achieve that closeness I so desired. I set aside a day and retired to the woods to spend the whole day and night in prayer, if necessary. Upon choosing my spot, I prayed with all the fervor of my soul. I really opened up and prayed, pleaded, suggested, and talked until there was no more left for me to say. I had said it all. I was empty of thought and word. Realizing that this effort had taken only a few minutes of my allotted twenty-four hours, I wondered what I should do for the rest of the day. Finally I decided that no revelations would come to such as I, and I returned home.

President David O. McKay knew well my type: "There are too many of us content to dwell in the slums of the intellect and of the spirit. Too many of us seek for happiness in the sunless surrounding of indulgence" (*Man May Know for Himself,* 186).

Shortly our branch became a ward, and I became the bishop. At a stake meeting, one of the bishops told how he had devoted an hour each day to prayer during the previous week. So moving was his spirit, so great his experience, that my soul desired this same joy. I vowed to myself that the next day would find me in an hour of prayer for myself, my family, my ward, and my job. But the next day was Sunday, and bishopric meeting was at 6:00 A.M. To arise early enough, I would have to get up at 4:00 A.M. My resolve vanished in sleep and fled to the corner of unfulfilled promises.

With my resolve renewed by a successful Sabbath, I set the alarm for Monday morning. As it rang, I sat up, put my feet on the floor, and attempted to rise. At once, and with great force, I was grabbed about the shoulders by a king-size mattress that pulled me forcibly back into its warmth and softness. I struggled valiantly for perhaps five or six seconds before I succumbed to its invitation. Then I gave up and slumbered on. After all, I consoled myself, I had become a bishop without any great sacrifice. I had my Duty to God Award; I'd been on a mission, married in the temple, paid my tithing, and had a temple recommend. How much additional spiritual guidance did I really need? I was a good, average, "natural" elder (see Mosiah 3:19).

The answer came from a young girl in our ward named Diana. She too had heard this talk on prayer and had put it to the test for an hour each day. One morning at a youth conference she bounded up to my wife and me, her face aglow and radiant with the light of the gospel as she bore witness to us of the greatness of a personal relationship and a daily communion with her Father. I thought, "How can I be a bishop of a ward if the members are praying harder than I am? How can I be a spiritual guide for them?"

The next morning found me in a small wooded area next to our home, where I poured out my heart to the Lord and meditated. Nearly an hour went by. The rewards were gratifying. As I prayed and talked and listened, a calmness of spirit and an inner warmth permeated my whole being, and my soul rejoiced. There were no heavenly messengers, no great lights, no visions or voices, but I felt myself lifted to new spiritual levels in that hour, and I knew I would never again be satisfied with a lesser effort in prayer.

Eventually, I retired to the meetinghouse each morning and there, with a chapter or two of the scriptures to stimulate my thinking to some serious meditation, I found myself pondering the things of the Spirit until I felt that I was ready to speak to my Father. Gradually, almost imperceptibly, I experienced the revelatory process Joseph Smith described, as strokes of pure intelligence entered my mind. Ideas for ward organization, solutions to family problems, new concepts for my seminary and institute classes, and a deep personal strength emerged daily and profusely from these prayers. I soon found that a pen and pad of paper were necessary to write down the ideas as they came. The promptings proved valuable as we reorganized our ward auxiliaries and issued call after call to people who, through the Spirit, knew of their new callings before they were made.

My family also benefited as their husband and father, a priesthood bearer, gave more inspired direction and counsel. Feelings of love and peace increased, and we rejoiced in new spiritual strength. My institute and seminary classes became more vibrant and interesting as I could see myself teaching more and more by the Spirit. The scriptures began to open up as never before, and I actually understood for the first time some of the writings of Isaiah that Jesus had told the Nephites were so valuable (see 3 Ne. 23:1–5).

But as great as was my joy, I found that I had not reached a final destination but was on a long and beautiful road that would lead to the fountain of living water—to Jesus, the source of all our knowledge, our faith, our truth, our being.

Anthony, "I Was a Bishop before I Really Learned to Pray," *Ensign*, Jan. 1976, 52.

If God, who has created you, . . . doth grant unto you whatsoever ye ask that is right, in faith, . . . O then, how ye ought to impart of the substance that ye have one to another.

MOSIAH 4:21

HE HANDED US AN ENVELOPE

JENN L. BRIAN

As a young mother I lived in a small house far away from the business parts of town. I had a few neighbors who lived nearby, but no stores, banks, libraries, doctors' offices, or any other such services were close.

Our family had only one car, and it was obviously wearing down. I knew it wasn't going to last much longer. To make things worse, the car was not big enough to hold our whole family anymore. We didn't have enough money to buy another car. Our existing car payment was very low but still very difficult for us to pay. We even had difficulty having enough money to buy groceries.

Our situation seemed hopeless. The only thing I knew how to do was pray for help.

I prayed every day, telling my Father in Heaven that I didn't know what to do about our transportation concerns and explaining that I needed his help. I had paid a full tithing for my entire life, and we were trying to be faithful. Based on our own resources, I could not see a way out. We simply needed help from on high.

One day a man we knew, who had no idea of our situation, called and asked if he and his wife could stop by to visit us in our home. At the time we already had some friends over, which we explained. The man gently persisted, saying they would stay only a few minutes.

My husband and I looked at each other with puzzled looks on our faces. We couldn't figure out why the other couple were anxious to come so quickly—particularly since they had to travel quite a distance.

After they arrived, they sat and talked to us briefly, talking about nothing of any great consequence. Then they stood up to leave. On their way out the door the man handed my husband an envelope.

After they left we opened the envelope and found a large sum of money. It was enough to make a substantial down payment on a used car, one big enough to hold our family. The amount of money we put down lowered the monthly payment so it was within our means.

A few days later I had an opportunity to speak to the man and his wife. I tried to thank them, but they explained that the money was not from them. A third party had given it to them to share with someone in need. The wife told me that her husband just couldn't get our family off his mind, and he knew the money was for us.

Within a month our old car was completely broken and not worth fixing, and we were able to buy a suitable replacement.

I am so grateful to Heavenly Father for hearing my pleadings and answering my prayers. I am also thankful to our anonymous helper, who selflessly made such a large donation to us, and to the man who came to our home, who was listening so closely to the Spirit that Heavenly Father was able to work through him to answer my prayer.

Whatsoever thing ye shall ask the Father in my name, which is good, in faith believing that ye shall receive, behold, it shall be done unto you.

MORONI 7:26

"REMEMBER THAT COOL TREASURE HUNT?"

DEBORAH STEVENS

One Christmas season we were particularly strapped for money. Some close friends had needed money to pay their rent; as we prayed about it we felt we should help them. We were then left with enough money to pay our tithing and bills and buy food, but we had very little for Christmas.

We also had little time to prepare for Christmas Day. My husband had a major project at work and frequently had to work late. I was busy with our three kids, expecting our fourth, and working part time from our home. We tried to be prayerful about our priorities, and it seemed that we never had time to go Christmas shopping. We asked the Lord to help us with both our time and money issues, trusting that he would somehow help us.

Finally we set out to try to find Christmas gifts for our children. It was two days before Christmas, and money was extremely tight. The kids needed new backpacks for school, and my husband found some good ones for a great price. I bought some things they really needed, including socks and underwear.

But I knew the kids wouldn't be very excited about receiving socks and underwear for Christmas, so I kept looking.

That was the year Pokémon cards were really big, and the stores had been sold out for a month. My kids really wanted some, but I figured that since it was so late in the season, they would just have to do without. As I looked around, I found some little gifts I thought the children would like, including some little Pokémon toys.

Then as I was walking down one aisle, I suddenly saw three packets of Pokémon cards, stashed out of place in an area where there were no Pokémon toys. I bought them, and I felt so thankful for this big blessing in a small package.

Now we had a few gifts, but they were very few. We wondered how we could make Christmas special for our children. Again we prayed for help, and a great idea came to us.

On Christmas Eve my husband and I created a treasure hunt for the kids to do on Christmas morning. At the end of the treasure hunt we hid their backpacks with Pokémon toys in one pocket and Pokémon cards in another pocket. The kids seemed more excited than normal as they rushed through the house finding clues that would lead them to their backpacks. They eagerly opened their cards and toys and played with them for a long time. They never said anything about not getting many other presents. They didn't even notice.

Now, years later, the kids say every Christmas, "Remember that Christmas when we had that cool treasure hunt? That was the best Christmas ever!" Then I feel grateful for wonderful kids and wonderful blessings from a loving Father who hears our prayers and helps us even in little things.

I did cry unto him and I did find peace to my soul.

ALMA 38:8

"I CLIMBED UP IN MY TREE HOUSE AND PRAYED"

KRISTINA SIMMONS

When I was ten years old, my father and I had a rather rocky relationship, in large part because we both had hot tempers. I recall one evening in particular when we got into a heated argument. I don't remember what we argued about, but I remember how I felt. I was boiling inside with fury. I could think of nothing else but our argument and how mad I was at my dad.

I was also upset because my best friend in all the world was coming for a short visit to our home. This friend had moved away a year before, and she was due to arrive any minute. I had been looking forward to her visit for weeks. I felt it would be the highlight of the whole year. I wanted to be able to play with her and enjoy our time together. But I was so upset that I knew our brief time together was going to be ruined. I tried to calm my inside rage, but I couldn't.

I went outside, climbed up in my tree house, and prayed. I pleaded for Heavenly Father to help me be in a good mood and not be so mad. I didn't fully understand that one of the roles of the Holy Ghost is to bless us with comfort. I didn't understand that Christ's atonement has power to help us change both our feelings and our behavior. What I did understand is that somehow Heavenly Father could help me.

I stayed there in the dark in my tree house for many minutes—praying and waiting. Gradually a feeling of peace filled my heart. When I finally climbed back down, I felt totally at peace—free of any anger. I went into our house and my friend was there. We played and talked and thoroughly enjoyed our time together. The time we were able to spend together that day was all I had hoped it would be. I was deeply grateful for the blessing I'd received from a Father in Heaven who heard and helped an angry little girl.

I look back on that experience as one that helped build my testimony as a young girl and helped me know and feel of God's love for me.

I don't know if I inherited my hot temper from my father, or if instead I learned it from him as I grew. But I must add, as a postscript, that through prayer and much effort, the Lord helped me conquer many of those tendencies over the years, and he helped me learn how to deal with my father in a calmer and much more respectful way.

Turn away . . . from doing thy pleasure
on my holy day; and call the sabbath a delight,
the holy of the Lord, . . . not doing thine own ways,
nor finding thine own pleasure.

ISAIAH 58:13

A MOTHER'S FAITH

MARION D. HANKS

I heard a noble mother speak once in a stake conference in response to invitation. I'll never forget her. She and her husband and twelve-year-old son lived on a ranch fourteen miles away from the place where they worshiped every Sunday. Saturday night the telephone rang, and the twelve-year-old came to his mother with the news that it was Bruce Brown, who was asking if he could go with Bruce and another friend and their fathers on a hunting and shooting trip the next morning. He wanted to know what he should tell Bruce.

The mother, as she stood at the pulpit fighting a problem of a lump in the throat, said, "My first impulse was to respond: 'Of course you can't go. Tomorrow is the Sabbath; tomorrow morning is priesthood meeting and Sunday School, and you have obligations.' But I didn't say that." She said she was also tempted to say, "You wait till your father comes in and ask him. He'll have an answer for you." But she didn't say that, either.

Somehow, she found the wisdom and restraint and faith to say: "Son, you're twelve years old. You hold the priesthood of God. You can make up your own mind about that."

He turned away without another word; she went with a prayer in her heart—a prayer with which mothers and fathers, I testify, are familiar: "Lord, Lord, please"—to her own room and knelt down and talked with the Lord. Nothing more was said about the incident.

Father came in; the three of them had their family prayer, went to bed, awakened early the next morning, and prepared for and then went in to priesthood meeting and Sunday School. They parked their pickup truck across the street in a parking lot and were crossing toward the chapel when a truck drove by with guns slung in the window, snowmobiles in the back, and two boys and two laughing men in the front.

The lady at the pulpit then had her hardest moment. She said, "I had hold of the hands of my two men, and as the truck passed the one on the right said, almost inaudibly, 'Gee, I wish . . .' and my heart clutched a moment; then he finished: 'Gee, I wish I could have convinced Bruce that he and Bob ought to be in priesthood meeting this morning.'"

And then we found out the reason for the big lump in the speaker's throat. She said, "We've been particularly grateful we were able to be with him that Sabbath morning, because it was the last Sunday we had him in this world. He was killed in a farm accident that week."

Thank God for a mother's faith, for a mother's wisdom, and a mother's love. There is no more honored place than a mother's, and certainly no more sacred responsibility.

Hanks, *Bread upon the Waters*, 148–49.

Thou calledst in trouble, and I delivered thee.

PSALM 81:7

THE LOST CROWN

ORRIN CLARK THOMAS

In a dental laboratory, the work is always exacting and can sometimes be tedious. Our labors include making gold and ceramic crowns and bridges, creating the parts for implanting a tooth, fitting a small gold inlay, and making natural-looking dentures. Everything we create is customized for a specific mouth. Our dentist clients require the product to be perfect (or nearly so), and they often need our work to be completed very quickly. Things do not always go smoothly, and there are times when our schedule is challenged because of the many problems that can occur.

One day the tension was particularly high in the dental laboratory where I work. We had more to do than we had time for; deadlines were looming, and many dentists were anxious for our products. Each technician in our lab was doing his or her best so that our commitments could be met.

Suddenly Steve, who worked near me, exclaimed, "Oh, no!" We all looked up with a start.

During the procedure of polishing a gold crown on the

polishing wheel, Steve had snagged the crown, and the motion of the wheel had flipped it over his shoulder. His heart sank, as did ours. We all knew that this particular crown was due to be delivered in only one hour.

He looked all over and couldn't find it. One by one, each of us joined him in the search. The counters were cluttered with our work, and the floor had cabinetry, instruments, supplies, and electrical cords. We looked everywhere but had no success. We were getting discouraged.

As I continued to look for the lost crown, I realized that we needed more help. I slipped into a nearby storage room and humbly asked Heavenly Father if he would be willing to help us find the lost gold crown. I explained that this dentist was an important client for our lab, that he was expecting the crown in less than an hour, and that we had failed in all our efforts to find it.

As I prayed, I remembered that the room where the crown was lost had recently been modified to accommodate a sandblasting machine. The fine points of the remodeling had not been completed—the floorboard was not continuous in one spot.

I got a flashlight, knelt on the floor, and peered into a small hole between the bottom of the Sheetrock and the end of the floorboard. There seemed to be a glint of something back there. I then bent the end of a long wire and reached it into that tiny space, about five inches deep, and pulled out the lost gold crown.

Steve let out a whoop of delight. He carefully took the crown from me, completed the polishing, thoroughly cleaned it up, and delivered it on time.

Neither the dentist nor his patient ever knew that the successful delivery of the crown that day came as a result of a sincere, quiet prayer—a prayer that was answered by a loving God.

Her children arise up, and call her blessed.

PROVERBS 31:28

"PLEASE HELP HIM FALL ASLEEP"

TANDEA FORD

Motherhood has been harder than I ever could have imagined—and yet much more rewarding.

When my son, Levi, was a toddler he was very hard to put to bed. He never wanted to stop playing or to end the day to go to sleep. When I finally would pick him up to carry him to his bed, he would cry and cry.

I learned it was very important for Levi to take regular naps every day. If he missed his nap, he would fall asleep in the late afternoon and then wake up too close to bedtime. Then he would want to stay up late at night. But even if he got to bed late, he would still wake up at his normal time the next morning. As a result, he would be fussy for a whole day, and it would take a few days to adjust his schedule back to normal.

I also found that if I would lay down right beside him and stoke his arm or his cheek, he would fall asleep. I would lie there with my eyes focused on his eyes, watching for any sign of a blink. And then would come longer blinks. And then total closure of his eyes. Even then, it took a few more minutes until I could slowly sit up and move out of his bed and tiptoe out of his room undetected.

Levi's big sister, who was four, did not fully understand how hard it was to get Levi to go to bed. Sometimes she didn't remember to stay out of the room and be quiet while I was putting Levi down for his nap. If she came in or made any loud noise at all, Levi would sit straight up, his eyes wide open. Then the whole "going to sleep routine" would start all over again.

Sometimes it was hard for me to take the time this process required. I felt overwhelmed with the tasks moms face every day, such as dishes, laundry, food preparation, the care of my daughter, and a myriad other things. I felt I didn't have enough time or energy to do all of it.

Because of this, sometimes I would lay in that toddler bed as tense as I could be. Sometimes it was all I could do to lie there stroking, looking at his eyes, and praying, "Please help him fall asleep, please make him sleep soon, please help him fall asleep . . ."

One day as I lay there holding my breath, hoping Levi would fall asleep soon, and praying, "Please help him fall asleep," I stopped and changed my prayer. "Heavenly Father, please help me be patient."

What I felt then was like a smile in my heart. It seemed that Heavenly Father said back to me, "Now you are praying for the right thing!"

He was telling me that doing the dishes, preparing lunch, and all those many other things I thought were so important could wait, because right then I was in the best place I could be. Where else on earth was better than that little bed at that moment, cuddled up to my most precious boy?

He was telling me I could choose to stop feeling tense, to let go of my mental "to do" list, to treasure the moment, and to be patient.

I am thankful to know that the most important things about being a mother are not whether my floor is swept or my flower beds are weeded. Much more important is that I hold tight to every tender moment.

It is important that I get certain things done each day. It is even more important that I make choices that will help my heart to grow.

Heavenly Father helps me focus on the joys of being a mom instead of letting myself get caught up in the burdens.

I know now I can choose moments like naptime to engulf my children with love and taste the sweet childhood spirit that all children have.

Faith and repentance bringeth a change of heart unto them.

HELAMAN 15:7

"WHY DON'T YOU *REALLY* PRAY ABOUT IT?"

H. BURKE PETERSON

In spite of the wall we build in front of us, when we cry out to the Lord, he still sends his messages from heaven; but instead of being able to penetrate our hearts, they hit the wall that we have built up and bounce off. His messages don't penetrate, so we say, "He doesn't hear," or "He doesn't answer." Sometimes this wall is very formidable, and the great challenge of life is to destroy it, or, if you please, to cleanse ourselves, purifying this inner vessel so that we can be in tune with the Spirit.

Let me give you some examples. I suppose we have all had someone do something to us that we didn't like, and that made us angry. We can't forget it, and we don't want to be around that person. This is called being unforgiving. Now, the Lord has had some very strong words to say to those who will not forgive one another. Many years ago I had an experience with being unforgiving. I felt I had been taken advantage of, and I did not like the person. I did not want to be around him; I would pass on the other side of the street if he came down it; I wouldn't talk to him. Long after the issue should have been closed, it was still cankering my soul. One day my wife, who is very astute and knows when I'm not doing everything I should, said, "You don't like so and so, do you?"

"No, I don't," I said. "But how could you tell?"

"Well, it shows—in your countenance it shows. Why don't you do something about it?" she said.

"Like what?"

"Why don't you pray about it?"

I said, "Well, I did pray once, and I still don't like him."

"No," she said, "why don't you *really* pray about it?"

Then I began to think, and I knew what she meant. So I decided that I was going to pray for a better feeling about this person until I had one. That night I got on my knees, and I prayed and opened up my heart to the Lord. But when I got up off my knees, I still didn't like that person. The next morning I knelt and prayed and asked to have a feeling of goodness toward him; but when I finished my prayers, I still didn't like him. The next night I still didn't like him; a week later I didn't like him; and a month later I didn't like him—and I had been praying every night and every morning. But I kept it up, and I finally started pleading—not just praying, but pleading.

After much prayer, the time came when without question or reservation I knew I could stand before the Lord, if I were asked to, and that he would know that at least in this instance my heart was pure. A change had come over me after a period of time.

That stone of unforgiveness needs to be removed from all of us, if it happens to be there, and I suggest that persistent prayer might be a way to remove it.

Peterson, "Prayer—Try Again," *Ensign*, June 1981, 73.

Lift up your heads and be of good comfort.

MOSIAH 24:13

"I WAS ALL USED UP"

ELAINE CANNON

Over the years, our family has had all manner of challenges as well as blessings in ways that have brought us to our knees in gratitude. There was a time when I was desperately ill and weakened from medication. My husband had suffered a critical stroke followed by a broken hip that left him wheelchair bound. Our children were living away from us. That meant that whenever we had to go to the doctor or anywhere else, I had to push him out to the car, support his transfer from the wheelchair to the car, lug the wheelchair into the trunk of our sedan, and then do it all again, in reverse, when we arrived. Each trip required such strenuous effort four times—out to the car, out of the car to the destination, back to the car, out of the car to our home. It was a demanding procedure that took a terrible toll on my already weakened and ill condition. In addition, because he hadn't worked for several years, our income had bottomed out. Not only was I spending much of my days caring for him, but I was also trying to support us with my freelance writing.

One morning I awakened feeling depressed and helpless,

wrestling with deep self-pity. I was convinced that God, my beloved God whom I had covenanted with and served, had forgotten me!

For several years I had been on my knees repenting of my weakness, pleading for our cause, explaining the problems of the six-foot-six cripple in my helpless care. I couldn't beg or bargain with God and struggle in faith anymore. I couldn't write another line. I couldn't handle one more trip to the doctor with my husband. I couldn't complain or share my feelings with my husband, who was sleeping soundly in his hospital bed down the hall. I was all used up and heartbroken beyond my ability to cope. Suddenly I wilted and wept. I could do no more. I couldn't even roll out of bed and kneel before a God I didn't feel close to anymore. Instead, I pulled the covers over my head and begged to die.

The next moment two things happened.

First, I felt a warm squeeze on my arm near my shoulder, just as my name was said in the voice of my long-dead, well-loved father.

Next, immediately, the telephone rang.

The caller identified himself. I knew him to be a very good man in our community, though personally we did not know him well. He apologized for such an early morning call, but he explained that he had been prompted by the Spirit to see how he could help us.

I was stunned and politely protested. He insisted. I was embarrassed. He was gentle but firm, saying that he could not hang up because the Spirit directing him to help us was too strong.

The outcome was that we were provided with a van equipped with a special passenger seat that moved out electrically to my husband's wheelchair, accommodated the transfer, and then moved him inside the car. It was wonderful.

Through that experience, a tender, valuable lesson was learned, and our lives changed. When my husband died, the van was passed along to another person in need of such convenience. All of this came because a man was in tune with the Spirit instead of being caught up in the fruits of his well-earned prestige. Yes, he had cast his net with great success in many ways over the years, but most important, he constantly sought to grow in stature before the Lord, as one of his disciples.

BOOKS CITED

Ayres, Kendall, ed. *Great Teaching Moments*. Salt Lake City: Bookcraft, 1990.

Brown, Hugh B. *Eternal Quest*. Salt Lake City: Bookcraft, 1956.

Burgess, Allan K. and Max H. Molgard. *Stories That Teach Gospel Principles*. Salt Lake City: Bookcraft, 1989.

Canfield, Anita R. *Remember, and Perish Not*. Salt Lake City: Bookcraft, 1998.

Christianson, Jack R. *What's So Bad about Being Good?* Salt Lake City: Deseret Book, 1992.

Hanks, Marion D. *Bread upon the Waters*. Salt Lake City: Bookcraft, 1991.

Hinckley, Gordon B. *Teachings of Gordon B. Hinckley*. Salt Lake City: Deseret Book, 1995.

Linford, Marilynne Todd. *Give Mom a Standing Ovation*. Salt Lake City: Bookcraft, 1996.

McKay, David O. *Man May Know for Himself: Teachings of President David O. McKay*. Clare Middlemiss, comp. Deseret Book, 1969.

Simmons, R. Scott. *Draw Near unto Me* (audiotape). Salt Lake City: Bookcraft, 1997.

Stoker, Kevin. *Missionary Moments*. Salt Lake City: Bookcraft, 1989.

Wright, Randal A. *Friends Forever*. Salt Lake City: Bookcraft, 1996.

SCRIPTURE INDEX

INDEX

ABOUT THE AUTHOR

Jay A. Parry has worked as an editor for the *Ensign* magazine, as a freelance writer, and as an editor for Deseret Book Company.

Brother Parry has served in The Church of Jesus Christ of Latter-day Saints as a stake president, a bishop, a high councilor, and as chair of a general Church curriculum writing committee.

A prolific writer, he has published *Everyday Heroes: True Stories of Ordinary People Who Made a Difference* and *Everyday Miracles: True Stories about God's Hand in Our Lives*. With Donald W. Parry as coauthor, he has published *Understanding Death and the Resurrection*, *Understanding the Signs of the Times*, *Understanding the Book of Revelation*, and *Understanding Isaiah*. He is also one of the creators and compilers of the successful "Best-Loved" series, which includes *Best-Loved Stories of the LDS People* (three volumes), *Best-Loved Poems of the LDS People*, *Best-Loved Humor of the LDS People*, and *Best-Loved Talks of the LDS People*.

He and his wife, Vicki Hughes Parry, are the parents of seven children and have five granddaughters.